D0597650

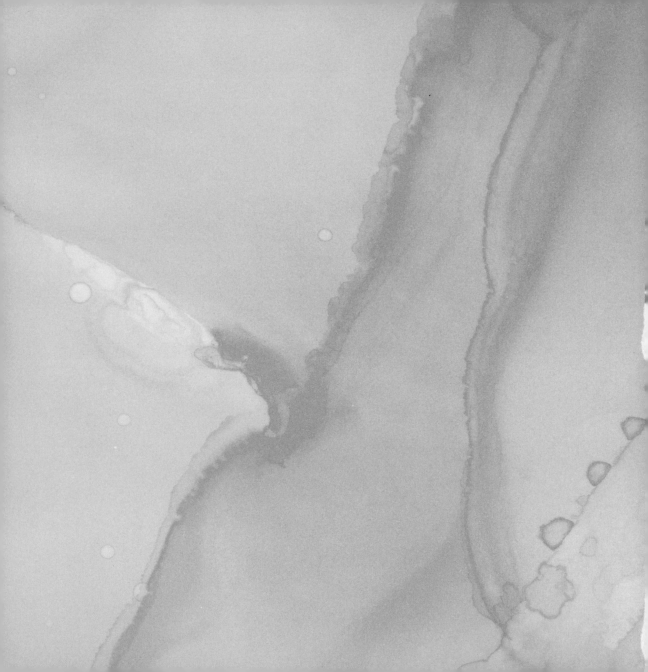

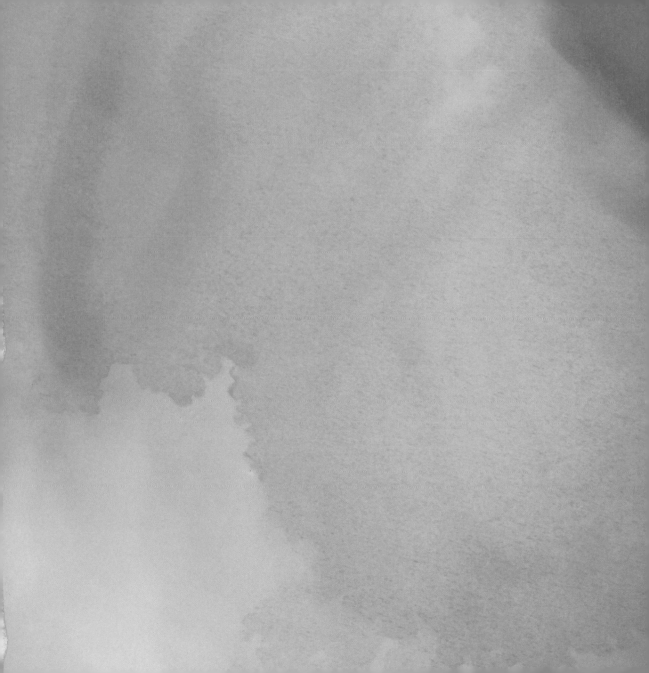

Brimming with creative inspiration, how-to projects, and useful information to enrich your everyday life, Quarto Knows is a favorite destination for those pursuing their interests and passions. Visit our site and dig deeper with our books into your area of interest: Quarto Creates, Quarto Cooks, Quarto Homes, Quarto Lives, Quarto Drives, Quarto Explores, Quarto Gifts, or Quarto Kids.

© 2019 Emily Silva

First published in 2019 by Rock Point, an imprint of
The Quarto Group, 142 West 36th Street, 4th Floor, New York, NY 10018, USA
T (212) 779-4972 F (212) 779-6058 www.QuartoKnows.com

All rights reserved. No part of this book may be reproduced in any form without written permission of the copyright owners. All images in this book have been reproduced with the knowledge and prior consent of the artists concerned, and no responsibility is accepted by producer, publisher, or printer for any infringement of copyright or otherwise, arising from the contents of this publication. Every effort has been made to ensure that credits accurately comply with information supplied. We apologize for any inaccuracies that may have occurred and will resolve inaccurate or missing information in a subsequent reprinting of the book.

Rock Point titles are also available at discount for retail, wholesale, promotional, and bulk purchase. For details, contact the Special Sales Manager by email at specialsales@quarto.com or by mail at The Quarto Group, Attn: Special Sales Manager, 100 Cummings Center Suite 265D, Beverly, MA 01915 USA.

Library of Congress Cataloging-in-Publication Data
Names: Silva, Emily, author.
Title: Find your glow, feed your soul / by Emily Silva.
Description: New York : Rock Point, [2019] | Includes
   bibliographical references and index.
Identifiers: LCCN 2019012246 (print) | LCCN 2019015558
   (ebook) | ISBN 9780760366134 (ebook) | ISBN
   9781631066412 (alk. paper)
Subjects: LCSH: Self-realization. | Spiritual life.
Classification: LCC BF637.S4 (ebook) | LCC BF637.S4 .S5483
   2019 (print) | DDC 158.1--dc23
LC record available at https://lccn.loc.gov/2019012246

10 9 8 7 6 5 4 3

ISBN: 978-1-63106-641-2

Publisher: Rage Kindelsperger
Creative Director: Laura Drew
Managing Editor: Cara Donaldson
Project Editor: Keyla Pizarro-Hernández
Art Director: Cindy Samargia Laun
Cover and Interior Design: Merideth Harte

Printed in China

This book provides general information on forming positive habits. However, it should not be relied upon as recommending or promoting any specific diagnosis or method of treatment for a particular condition, and it is not intended as a substitute for medical advice or for direct diagnosis and treatment of a medical condition by a qualified physician. Readers who have questions about a particular condition, possible treatments for that condition, or possible reactions from the condition or its treatment should consult a physician or other qualified healthcare professional. The author and publisher are in no way responsible for any actions of behaviors undertaken by the reader of this book.

FIND YOUR

glow

FEED YOUR

soul

A Guide for Cultivating a Vibrant Life of Peace & Purpose

EMILY SILVA

ROCK
POINT

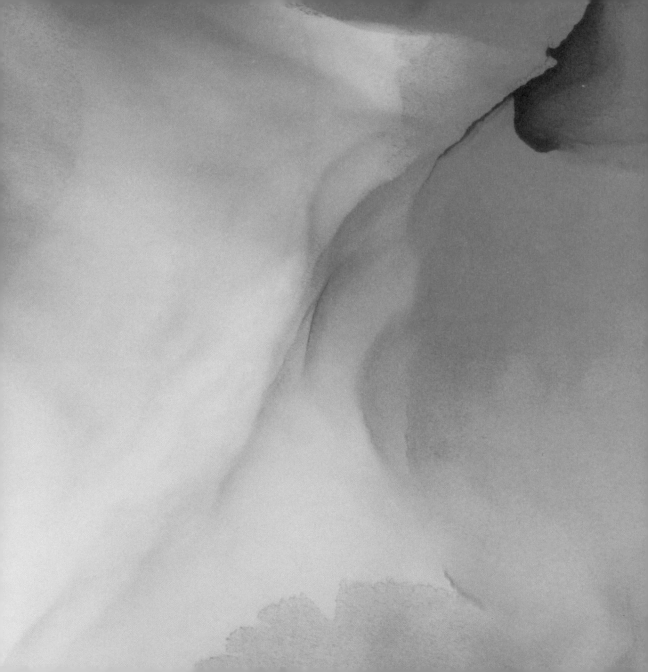

For my nieces: Dalleen, Alyssa, Grace, Lily, Kiah, and Mira.

May you always shine your lights and know how beautiful you are.

Table of Contents

"I wish I could show you
when you are lonely or in
darkness the astonishing
light of your own being."

—HAFIZ

INTRODUCTION

believe that every person has a light within them. Our lights are a source of inspiration, levity, and life. Learning to access our inner lights can bring better awareness to our own needs and desires and those of others. Finding your inner glow is a way to tap into one of your greatest sources of power: your soul.

You may ask, "What is my inner glow?" It is the part of you that shines even through hard times. It is when your soul feels truly alive. When this happens, your eyes brighten, smiles are effortless, and peace seems to reside where stress used to live. With an inner glow, we can illuminate dark places and bring warmth to situations that need understanding.

Paying attention to our inner glow invites joy, contentment, and love for ourselves and others. Sometimes we shine our lights so brightly that we seem to be abundant in love, connection, health, and ideas. At other times, our lights are dimmed for various reasons—such as grief, stress, anxiety, hardship—and it is at these times that it feels impossible to ignite our inner light. But it is important to note that we never lose our light, as it is always within us, ready to shine brightly.

There are several examples of glow in nature. Our solar system is full of light and glow. Stars continue to shine even on the darkest nights. Fireflies create magic sparks on summer nights. Even the tides can glow when the conditions are just right.

I am excited to take you on a journey to find your distinctive glow. Our glow is unique to each of us, just as the sun and moon glow differently, yet beautifully in their own way.

When we know how to access our inner light and are connected to it, we glow from the inside out.

Have you noticed that it is impossible to ignore someone who emanates light? They are magnetic and radiate warmth, and when they smile they beam from the inside and draw people towards them. Their eyes light up and they exude warmth. There is a vibrancy that is deeper than physical beauty, which draws people in.

Several years ago, I wanted to find ways to live my most vibrant life. I started to feel sluggish and not myself. Fatigue set in and I was determined to figure out ways to radiate from within. I was tired of feeling tired, so I went on a search for things to help me look and feel my best.

I learned that when we take care of ourselves from the inside, we emanate joy, love, peace, and power.

True happiness comes from finding inner peace and learning to be comfortable with ourselves and accept who we are, just the way we are.

Prioritizing self-care and paying attention to things that sap our energy is key to maintaining our inner glow. When we feed our souls, we can't help but glow.

This book is meant to be both an inspiration and a helpful tool to access your inner light. My hope is that by reading it you will find a renewed sense of love and you will make self-care a priority. This is an easy-to-use A–Z guide, and each chapter is a beacon to help you discover your inner glow, so you can give and receive acceptance, love, gratitude, and positivity.

There is a secret here:

When we find our inner glow, we glow on the outside too.

My intention is to encourage you to find what resonates and perhaps create an "inner glow" routine where you tap into your light daily until doing so becomes effortless. I use the word "universe" often to define the divine source that some may call "God," "Higher Power," "Spirit," etc., but please insert your preferred word as you read.

The following chapters come from my own personal experiences and from years of coaching women through personal and career growth transformations. I became a life coach after working for several years in corporate America. Although I was successful, I didn't feel fulfilled. I took the leap and left the security of my career to pursue what my soul was begging me to do: become a coach and author. My mission is to help women harness their bravery and use it to go after what they really want, because I know that until we are honest and brave, we can't live a life that is fulfilling. As a life coach, it has been my honor to be a part of these women's journeys, and I am grateful for every lesson that I have learned. I hope that you find something that resonates with you and brings more light into your beautiful life.

To glow from within takes consistent effort and awareness. Pay attention to the things that light you up and the things that sap your energy. Just knowing what these are can help tremendously when trying to keep your light shining bright.

Saying "yes" to things that light you up and "no" to light-dimmers is a step in the right direction.

I hope you find the tools in this book applicable to your unique situation. I understand that we are all from different situations and I appreciate our diversity; everything in this book might not apply to you, but I hope that something will and can help you find the joy, peace, and fulfillment you desire.

What I do know is that if we all work on glowing as brightly as possible we can make a beautiful difference.

By finding your inner glow, you are taking part in raising the vibrations of the planet.

To each reader, you are now part of a glow tribe. We are all connected by our desires to be our best selves and shine more light in this world—which needs it now more than ever. We must start with ourselves and then our lights can illuminate places that are dark, to spread love and hope that is desperately needed.

Thank you for choosing this book as part of your journey.

15

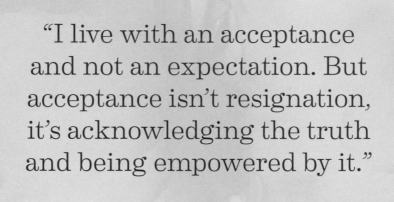

"I live with an acceptance
and not an expectation. But
acceptance isn't resignation,
it's acknowledging the truth
and being empowered by it."

—MICHAEL J. FOX

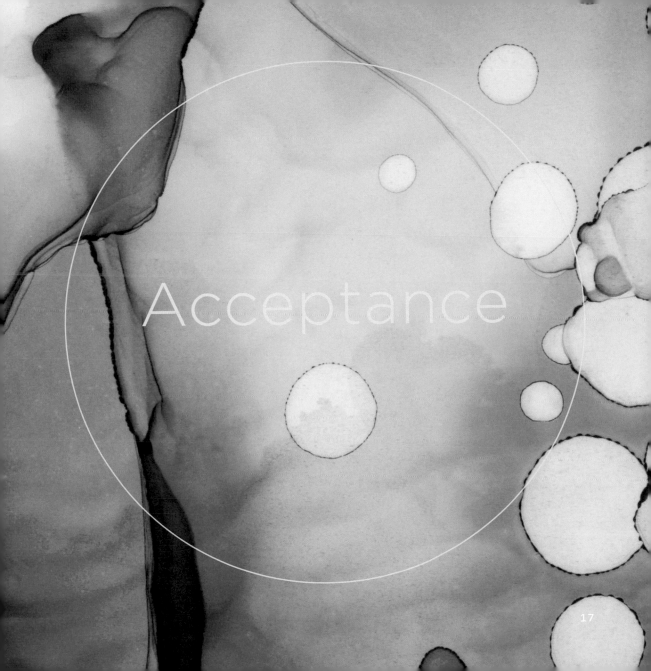

Acceptance

Acceptance is an act of release. Every day, we are faced with choosing whether to accept what is or resist and challenge it. Sometimes resistance is necessary to push through and grow, but other times, surrendering is needed to allow what is meant to be happen, and that is a difficult lesson. Knowing when to accept and when to resist requires awareness.

Our sparkle can become dull if we resist when surrender is needed. Stress seeps in, we begin to worry, and the need to control becomes obsessive. Our bodies react to the tension, leaving us uneasy and in discomfort. When these physical symptoms are present, it is a cue to release and accept. Acceptance allows us to experience the flow of life, which opens us up to greater understanding.

Dealing with disappointments in your life, career, or relationships can make you believe that expectations leave little room for acceptance—especially when you fiercely hold on to what you think is supposed to happen in your life. When your expectations aren't met, you can often feel you have no choice but to struggle and fight. Trying to live up to unrealistic expectations, that can cause symptoms of depression or anxiety, begins to take over your life. But sometimes accepting your circumstances, learning from them and moving on is more beneficial to one's well-being.

When we allow the struggle to stay real and we resist the lesson that is begging to be learned, we can find ourselves with our arms open, crying to the universe:

"I'm letting go now! Please help me move forward."

I seem to repeat this prayer often. And you know what? It is answered each time. But the thing is, the way it is answered is not always how we may envision, and this is where we learn the beautiful lesson of acceptance, and that we should surrender to the flow of life.

The beautiful thing is that on the other side of resistance there is a new plan that we may not have visualized. When we surrender to the new reality, everything inside of us can relax. We can breathe again, and our thoughts are no longer hijacked by the anxious grip of control.

The less we resist, the easier things become.

When you cry out to the universe, it hears you. In fact, it knows exactly what you need, which is probably why such prayers are uttered from our core, in moments of desperation and anxiety. It is like we try to hold on with every bit of control until we are left hanging, desperate to find stability once more.

And then the answers come in, sometimes in a trickle and sometimes in a flood.

When the answers arrive, acceptance can begin. In order to fully accept there must be an element of remembering where you were before the prayer was lifted. The ego most often loves this tender spot; it can accept the temporary relief and decide to take over once again. This is not full acceptance, though. Full acceptance is a great release of the need to control and ability to sink into the flow of life.

One of the hardest lessons to learn is to accept things the way they are and let go of expectations. This is a struggle. It is easy to place expectations on the outcome because we want what we want, but when we set expectations, we open ourselves up to disappointments.

Acceptance is an act of receiving; there is no control here, only openness.

Acceptance

To learn how to accept what is, we need to identify areas of frustration in our lives—the areas in which we desire to have control. It's best to break this down into internal and external factors. Here are a few examples:

Internal

- Body image
- Negativity
- Resentments
- Judgements

External

- Career
- Relationships
- Friendships
- Family
- Community

When you identify the internal and external factors that are causing frustration, ask yourself, "What can I change about this?" Even if the answer is something small, take a step towards making that change. Then whatever you can't change, release the desire to control and surrender by accepting.

This is often easier said than done. Control is intoxicating and there is nothing better than getting what we want. The ego can be very loud when acceptance is necessary. However, the peace that follows acceptance far outweighs the illusion of control.

Acceptance invites a state of flow into our lives. Allowing things to flow in and out as they are meant to rids us of the pain of resistance. Resistance breeds anxiety and worry; acceptance allows peace to enter and frees us from the pain of struggle.

Imagine letting go of a worry and watching it float away into the ether, like a balloon. As you watch it fly higher and higher, you feel lighter. The weight of control is lifted and the hands that once held on so tightly to it are now free to receive whatever is next. Once the balloon drifts from your view, feel your worry disappear with it. Breathe in the relief.

This weightlessness is available on the other side of control. When the answers arrive, squelch the desire to control by offering gratitude and acceptance. Practice openness, and when anxiety wells up, it is a cue that something no longer serves your soul. Release it and make room for your inner glow to shine once more. Accept whatever you need to enter your life.

All will be well.

"If we have no peace, it is because we have forgotten that we belong to each other."

—MOTHER TERESA

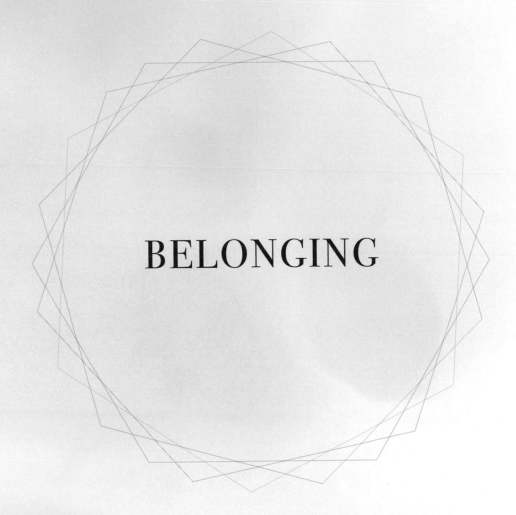

BELONGING

Longing to belong is a common human emotion because we are built for connection. When we feel we don't belong, our hearts ache as if something is missing. Belonging brings understanding, compassion, and community into our lives. It feels good to be part of a group of individuals who share a common goal, interest, or even bloodline. We each define our personal need to belong on our own terms, and once we find that sweet spot, it feels like our soul has found a home.

Belonging is such a wonderful feeling, and we can find it within our families and communities, or even create a tribe of our own.

Once we find and feel true belonging, we light up and open our hearts to others in the group.

This openness allows our hearts the freedom to be fully expressive and feel the connection we crave.

Finding a group of like-minded individuals can take some time, especially while our ideals and beliefs are taking shape and solidifying. For many of us, we can find our tribe in high school or even college. Some of us gain a sense of belonging in our careers or spiritual communities. Belonging is available in many places; the key is getting clear on what that means and feels like to you.

I spent a good portion of my 20s and early 30s moving around and traveling all over the world for work; I made friendships, but my soul longed for deeper connections. I noticed that I wasn't staying in one place long enough to form a tribe or sense of community. Although it was easy to meet people, I found myself sharing the same introductory information about myself but never diving deeper.

Have you ever felt tired of sharing the same information repeatedly in the hope of finding a connection or community that feels right? It's frustrating to get your hopes up when you meet a potential friend only to have him or her drop off after one or two meet-ups. Finding a tribe is almost like dating. In this age of endless choice, it is easy to fill our calendars with social events, yet we find it difficult to actually build substantial relationships. Creating a deeper connection requires more than pleasantries.

Trust is built in the moments shared, the little things, and by consistently showing up and being there for each other, whether that is close by or from afar.

I realized that my constant movement was keeping me from forming the types of connections I was craving.

One of the ways to find your tribe is to open your heart and put down roots.

By staying in one place you can focus on nurturing relationships and finding the people you resonate with.

This can be done by taking a class, volunteering, participating in community activities, joining a gym, or a sports league. All of these activities help us find others with similar interests, and when we put down roots, we become reliable.

Even if we move and put down roots in a new place, our closest friends can still live miles away. Technology has become key to keeping these relationships thriving. It is now easier than ever to stay connected to our important connections who live far away. A tribe does not necessarily have to live near each other; there must be common threads of love, compassion, and respect to link everyone together.

Putting down roots and making the effort to stay connected to faraway friends is a great place to begin to find a sense of belonging and in understanding what is important to you when it comes to feeling that sense of belonging. Being honest about what you need from a tribe begins with considering some important questions surrounding trust, respect, and love.

BELONGING

If you want to identify or create your tribe, think about your own relationships and ask yourself the following questions:

- Does this person encourage me to be the best version of myself?

- Is there a spirit of love?

- Do we align on ideals and respect each other's differences?

- Are we honest with each other, even when it's difficult?

- Do they inspire and provide light during my dark times, and vice versa?

When you identify the people in your life who provide the care, support, and understanding that you desire, take some time to offer gratitude for each of them. Send them a card, text or call them to express your love and gratitude. Keep the effort of connection alive and it will return to you.

If you can't identify one person who exemplifies "tribe" for you, consider who you are spending your time with. Is now the moment to move on from a certain social scene or habits? If you want to attract something into your life, you need to show up as that person as well as make space for what is meant to be.

Let go of anything that doesn't light you up or that weighs you down. Our souls long to belong and we are wired for it. We must feed this desire in our souls. By taking some time to get clear on what you want out of a community and your relationships, you can better identify where you need to go, how you need to show up and open up to connection. In time, your tribe will form and the effort it took will be worth it. If you have found your tribe, do something to deepen the connection and show your gratitude for their role in your life.

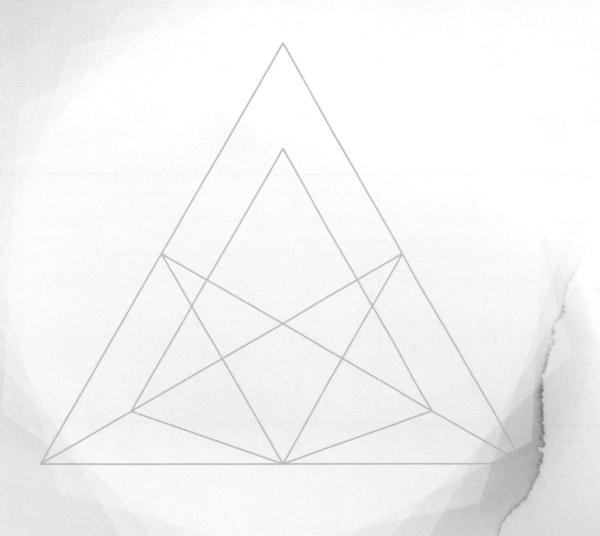

"The more you praise and celebrate your life, the more there is in life to celebrate."

—OPRAH WINFREY

CELEBRATE
YOUR WINS

You deserve to acknowledge and celebrate your accomplishments. You are capable of doing some pretty amazing things that deserve recognition and praise. Celebrating can be a form of offering gratitude to yourself for the hard work that goes into a project, completing a task that seemed impossible, and even for the little things that get you to where you want to be in life.

However, it can be hard to accept praise for accomplishments and celebrate wins. It can feel selfish and prideful, and many of us back away from the attention of celebration. But it is important to recognize your efforts and cultivate self-confidence because it helps you understand your value and cultivates joy.

Taking time to celebrate your wins is healthy and opens your eyes to all the amazing experiences life provides.

Valuing the wonderful things in life opens our eyes to all there is to celebrate. At first it may feel strange to celebrate yourself, but in time you will see just how much greatness there is in your own life and all around you.

Celebration breeds joy and gratitude. When we take the time to feel the satisfaction of a win and offer gratitude to ourselves, there is a shift within. Think about how celebrating makes you feel; there is excitement, smiles, pride, and value placed on the situation.

In fact, celebrating is an act of love. When we celebrate other people, we are happy for them; we extend love by way of showing up, spending time with them, and sometimes by bringing gifts, too. Each of us deserves this love.

When you celebrate yourself, you are offering yourself love.

I noticed that I had a hard time with this and wanted to learn how to let go of this fear. To get over my aversion to celebrating, I made a list of all of my accomplishments and how I celebrated them. This was enlightening. I noticed that I had a pattern of accomplishing something and then moving on rather quickly to the next achievement. No wonder I had anxiety around celebrating—I wasn't taking time to reflect, rest, and celebrate!

Fear of celebration might sound silly, but once I started my coaching business, I realized just how many women struggle with this issue. The common theme usually came from fellow overachievers, who once they achieved something tended to just move on to the next thing. This seems to be because, internally, we are always competing with ourselves. This spiral of competition never gives us the time to "rest on our laurels" and sit in the reality of what we have just accomplished.

Other reasons included not wanting to draw attention to themselves because they were shy and not feeling that what they had accomplished was "good enough." As we worked on creating ways to celebrate their wins, their confidence went up, their self-worth was embraced, and joy emerged as they realized the significance of their accomplishments.

A SPIRIT OF CELEBRATION

I love hearing about what my clients have accomplished and are proud of. It is wonderful to celebrate with them and recognize how they are becoming more comfortable sharing their wins. Some of the common themes are:

- Buying a house

- Starting a business

- Letting go of a toxic relationship

- Losing weight

- Adopting a puppy

- Graduating college

- Having a baby

- Finally getting rid of clutter

- Running a mile without stopping

When was the last time you achieved something that you had been working towards? Think about how you reacted to the completion of the goal. Did you share it with anyone? It is important to recognize your accomplishments. I encourage you to take some time to create your own list and note how you celebrated each success. Make sure you include everything that you are proud of.

Let go of the fear and judgement and open up to the idea of celebrating your list of wins.

To further develop a spirit of celebration, take a moment each day to find something that you are proud of accomplishing. There are so many things to celebrate in our daily lives, such as learning something new, making a friend, beating the traffic home, or cooking an amazing meal. Our small daily wins are worth noting and celebrating.

Try to make it a point to create celebrations for every win big and small. You will begin to notice that an attitude of celebration creates more joy and a sense of healthy pride in your life, therefore cultivating your inner glow.

It is important to be able to acknowledge and share your wins because you deserve to be celebrated. I encourage you to create a celebration for yourself to appreciate everything you have done. Make sure you look back on your entire life and write down anything that went unnoticed that you feel deserved acknowledgement. It's never too late to give yourself the acknowledgement you desire. Even better, do this exercise with a friend and celebrate each other's wins together. Collective joy is contagious.

Life is beautiful, and too short not to take a pause to enjoy all that is incredible.

"If the only prayer you ever say in your entire life is 'thank you,' it will be enough."

—MEISTER ECKHART

Daily Gratitude

Gratitude is a powerful action and feeling that we can nurture daily. The act of practicing daily gratitude creates room for more gratitude to occur and brings more joy into our lives. When we calibrate our brains to look for things to be grateful for, we tune into the abundance of life.

Gratitude replaces scarcity with enough, it generates appreciation, creates a positive outlook, and is excellent for our health.

Feeling grateful reduces feelings of stress, anxiety, and depression. In order to access these benefits, we need to invite gratitude into our lives and practice it every day.

For several years, practicing gratitude has been a daily habit for me, and I have noticed changes in my outlook, overflowing blessings, and a more open heart because of it. It is remarkable how the simple act of saying or writing, "I am grateful for…" can create a shift in perspective. Ever since I started this practice, the smallest things—like a tiny flower blooming in the weeds or the shapes of clouds in the sky—bring me joy because my mind is calibrated to see the good in everything.

Practicing gratitude does not take extra time and is not difficult to incorporate into your daily routine. You can do it when you wake up, when you eat, on your commute, and—my favorite—right before bed. One way to do this is to reflect on the day's activities and think of at least three things that you're grateful for.

A gratitude journal is an amazing and effective tool to create a daily gratitude habit.

Write down something that you are grateful for each day. Try to find three to five things each time as your practice grows. Some days will be harder than others, but on those challenging days, it is even more important to stay dedicated to your practice. Pushing through the discomfort will get you to the other side where appreciation and joy reside.

Reviewing your gratitude journal from a particularly rough day or reading through past entries when you are having a difficult time can help transform thoughts of scarcity and defeat into thoughts of abundance and victory. This is can be an excellent reminder of all the goodness that has occurred in your life—big and small— and you will gain immense gratitude and pleasure from this exercise. It is difficult to maintain a negative mindset when you remind yourself of all the things you are grateful for.

And there are so many things to be grateful about. To begin: the food we eat, the air we breathe, the clothes we wear, having a place to live, our homes. Offer thanks to the universe for the opportunities it provides and to the people who make an impact on your life. Every day you will notice that there is always something or someone to be grateful for.

Creating a daily practice can change your mind, body, and soul by infusing positivity.

Positive thoughts have a higher vibrational frequency and will attract like energy into our lives. When our output is grateful, it is amazing how many more things occur that we can be grateful for.

Giving thanks can also raise the vibrations that might have been lowered as a result of recent difficult events. Even on the worst days, you will notice that gratitude transforms your energy throughout the day. During hard times, we can change the energy of our day by taking a moment to find something positive.

Whether you begin or end your day with gratitude, you will notice a change in perception over time.

When I began my practice, one of the first things I noticed was how bright and orange California poppies are. It was such a simple thing to notice but the memory is a distinct one for me. California poppies are the state flower; they are a vibrant orange and can be found all over the state during the spring. I have lived in California my entire life and yet I have never stopped to appreciate the vibrancy of these flowers.

As I was waiting to get onto a highway one day, I looked over and was amazed at the shock of orange bursting from the ground surrounding the sign post. I did a double take and realized that something so ordinary had become extraordinary for me. I felt grateful for this observation and my new-found attention to everyday things.

As my outlook changed, I realized that I had calibrated my mind for gratitude.

We can intentionally create a change through consistent practice. Our brains can create new pathways with the practice of a new skill such as exercise, meditation, or diet. Practice creates muscle memory. Have you ever noticed how we can remember something even after not doing it for a while? As long as we practice, the activity becomes familiar. Over time, practicing gratitude creates more thoughts and occurrences for gratefulness.

Not only will you create a more positive outlook, and reduce feelings of stress and anxiety, but you will also sleep better. When gratitude is practiced before bedtime you switch out focus from the day's stresses and become more relaxed. Sleeping better helps you to be more productive during the day and improves your mood.

This practice alone will impact your inner glow quickly because focusing on being grateful replaces disgruntled and frustrated emotions with joy and contentment. If we can choose gratitude every day, we can redirect the negative emotions that may have come up during the day with ease.

I encourage you to begin practicing gratitude. Try it for four weeks and see what transpires. Start a gratitude journal and write down one, three, or five things that you are grateful for each day, and you will soon notice the gradual change in your perception.

A grateful heart glows because it operates at a high vibration, which increases your radiance.

As you deepen your practice, you will begin to attract even more things to be grateful for because your mind will be calibrated to seek them out and take notice.

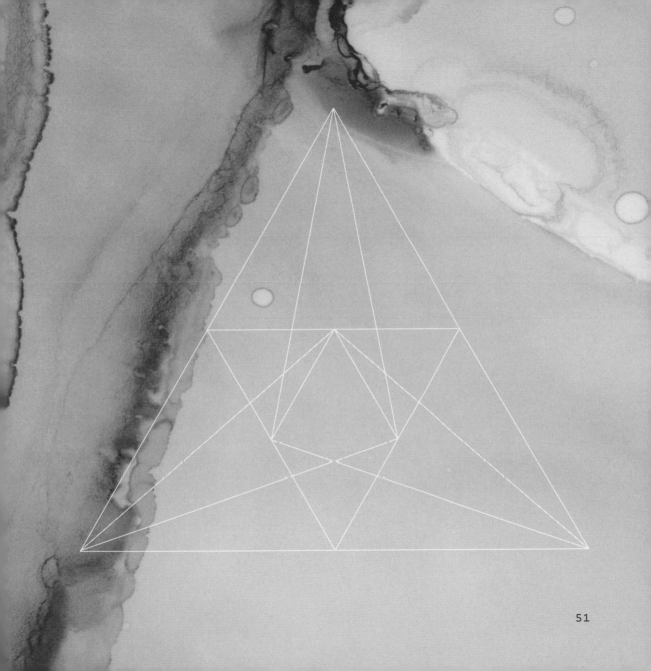

"Your task is not to seek for love,
but merely to seek and find all
the barriers within yourself that
you have built against it."

—RUMI

Embody Love

Everyone desires love—it is one of our deepest needs—this is evident the moment we are born and it never ceases as we age. So many things could be solved if we were all just more loving. Love is complex because it carries with it the need for acceptance and belonging, and many times our hurt feelings create barriers within us that keep us from giving and receiving love.

Sometimes we build walls around our hearts to protect us against getting hurt, however, these barriers keep us from experiencing and embodying love. If there is something you want badly enough, the secret is to embody it.

If you want more love in your life, you need to be loving.

This lesson can be hard, especially after years of heartbreaks and disappointments. It can be scary to put your heart out there again, afraid to be hurt. Cynicism can set in, and your faith in finding a good partner may be fading. You may even begin to feel the comfort of solitude once more and wonder if there is someone out there meant for you.

When we learn to love ourselves and treat ourselves with the respect we deserve, our energy shifts and our hearts open up. An open heart is the first step to attracting more love. If we keep the walls and our guard up, no one—not even you—will be able to penetrate it.

Once our hearts begin to open, we can get a crystal-clear idea as to what it is that we really want. This will be different for everyone, so going inward and discovering what your heart truly desires is key to figuring out how to love yourself and the way in which you need to be loved.

When you step back from the situation, ask yourself if you really know what you want and if you are loving yourself in the way that you want to be loved? Release any expectations you may have. Expectations create a sense of control that will cause greater stress.

The first thing to do is to create the heart space for love to re-enter. In order to do this, make a list of what you really want and what is most important to you, then start visualizing it daily. When it comes to finding your person, see yourself with him or her and notice how it feels to be in his or her presence. At first it might feel silly to sit and visualize a person that you aren't sure exists, but as you dig deeper into what you really want, you will begin to actually see and feel it happening.

Then, work on emulating what you desire. If you want a loving relationship, you need to be loving. Begin by bringing love to every situation in your life, including with yourself.

Self-love should become a priority.

The more you embrace yourself for who you are and work on embodying love in other areas of your life, the more you will notice cynicism and doubt being replaced with hope and faith that you will find the love you desire. Once you know what you want and how you want to be loved, take the time to nurture and love yourself.

In order to truly give and receive love, we have to give love to ourselves. It's amazing how our critical mind quiets when we flood it with approval and love. Try to catch the negative thoughts as they come and replace them with love and approval. It's a practice but just trying to give and receive love makes a difference.

CULTIVATE
Giving Love

First, you have to believe that you are worthy of love. If you want to blossom and thrive in love, take some time to create more love for yourself by giving love to yourself and others.

- Notice what you do love about yourself and celebrate these things.

- Notice what you love in others instead of allowing comparison to creep in.

- Take time for self-care which can include exercise, eating healthy, setting goals or journaling.

- Say "thank you" when you receive a compliment. This is an energetic way to remind yourself that you are worthy of love.

By taking these steps to embody love, you will start to feel more loving and it will become easier to receive and give love.

Trust that the universe knows
exactly who you need in your life
and release control.

Soon after doing this work, I met my husband. When I think back on all the struggles, heartaches, and tears before meeting him, I see that I was pushing something to happen that I wasn't really clear on. With clarity and intentional focus, everything else was brushed aside. There was no questioning or anxiety when it came to him and so we came together naturally.

Getting to know and falling in love with him has been one of the greatest adventures of my life. When I decided that I was going to get clear on what I wanted, I opened my eyes, mind, and heart to whatever that would be. I allowed the manifestation to take place at the right time with the right person.

By deciding to embody love, I opened
up to whatever was supposed to occur.

Self Love

If you would like to invite more love into your life, here is an exercise you can do to create a deeper connection with your heart:

- Answer the three questions posed below:

  ¤ What are my top three qualities?

  ¤ What is my favorite thing about myself?

  ¤ What am I most proud of?

- Hold your hand over your heart and feel your heartbeat

- As you feel your heartbeat, breathe in your top three qualities as you say them out loud

- Offer your body love and gratitude. Thank your heart for beating and pumping blood through your entire body. Thank your legs for taking you places. Thank your mind for all the work it does. Thank your soul for your unique personality.

Finally, mantras are a great way to open your heart and invite love in. Whether you are single, in a relationship, getting out of a relationship, or in the "it's complicated" camp, take a moment to repeat this heart-opening mantra:

My heart is open, and I am ready to receive love.

Sit with your palms up, which is a receptive pose; open to receiving the answers on how you want to receive love. Be willing to accept love and repeat this mantra daily. An open heart is a beautiful thing. It's amazing what takes place when we are open and ready to receive.

You can always come back to this place of love, acceptance, and gratitude. We teach others how to treat us, so we might as well love ourselves with abandon. If you want fierce love, learn to give and receive it from yourself. It is from a place of complete love and acceptance of ourselves that we can then give love and shine from the inside out.

"Offering forgiveness prevents us from being destroyed by a corrosive resentment. It helps us grow in being magnanimous."

—DESMOND TUTU

FORGIVENESS

One of the hardest things to do, but probably the most healing, is to forgive, especially when the hurt is deep. Forgiveness may not be instantaneous and sometimes we need to forgive multiple times, but it is better to do this than hold on to the hurt, letting bitterness fester.

There is a beautiful release that comes with forgiveness.

When you allow your soul to release pain and bring love back to where pain resides, healing occurs.

You don't have to try to forget the painful action or have that person over for dinner, forgiveness is a gift to yourself. There is power in just releasing the energy of anger and resentment. Forgiveness releases the chains of pain from your heart and soul so that love and healing can take place.

Bring hope, love, and forgiveness to your wounds. Allow wisdom to grow where pain once resided. Our wounds can become a source of wisdom. When we bring forgiveness and understanding to a painful situation, we open ourselves up to become a wounded healer; allowing our wounds to bring healing and become an inspiration to others.

The beautiful thing about forgiveness is that our souls become more resilient when we are able to release the grip of something as strong as hurt and resentment. In fact, many times we can hold on to the pain when the offending party has already moved on, leaving us in a victim state, stripped of our power.

There have been many events that have offered me the opportunity to practice forgiveness; broken hearts, familial situations, disappointments at work, and friendships falling apart. I have felt hurt and disregarded, and realized that despite my pain, I had to learn how to forgive in order to release myself from the pain I was holding on to.

Through these lessons, I learned that we all have different levels of understanding, and that was where many of these problems stemmed from. The need to be right, understood, and validated may never happen in a situation, so instead of dwelling on the anger of the misunderstandings I realized that I had to release the need to be right and understood and forgive instead.

Sometimes people will never understand or agree with us, even if they are completely wrong or out of line.

Releasing our pain by offering forgiveness gives us the freedom to heal and move on.

Sometimes we need to let go of the entire relationship and sometimes we just need to bring compassion and grace to a situation. When anger and resentment feel like they are taking over, compassion and grace are key to understanding. If we hold on to bitterness, we will be stuck in a cycle of pain.

When a disagreement occurs, it is hard to come back together when hurt and resentment arise. If the relationship is important to you and the foundation is love, be the first to bridge the gap of pain. Go first. Soften. Offer forgiveness.

Give love where love is needed. Apologize. Be brave and offer grace. Healing occurs when resentment doesn't have time to grow the roots of bitterness; that is what forgiveness does, it breaks you free from the grip of anger, resentment, and bitterness.

In order to heal, offer compassion even though you may not fully understand the extent of the other person's pain. You have a choice: forgive or hold on to resentment.

With time, the relationship may be restored. If not, you will give yourself a gift of the dissipation of the bitterness that you had harbored through the practice of forgiving and letting go. Bitterness will only damage and hurt your soul and eat away at your heart. Forgiveness is the only way to truly let go of all the hurt and pain and allow your soul to glow as it is intended.

An effective way to begin this process is to write a letter stating all the pain and hurt you have experienced. Let the person know how hurt, angry, disappointed, betrayed, and sad their actions or a situation made you feel. Then try to offer understanding and forgiveness. Let them know that you are releasing the pain and you forgive them for the hurt they caused. Finally, tear this letter up and release it all. The pain no longer serves you.

Sometimes that letter will be addressed to yourself. Self-forgiveness is needed many times and going through this exercise for yourself is also healing.

Release the attachment to the pain and give yourself understanding, forgiveness, and love.

Sometimes there isn't reconciliation and the realization that a relationship is beyond repair is tough. It is hard to accept that someone you have been close to for a long time has started to grow apart from you. It can feel like a branch splitting and creating two new trees. Each tree is growing and blossoming, but separately. It hurts to lose someone you are close to. Anger, resentment, confusion, and sadness happen all at once. Releasing the pain over time, after forgiveness has taken place, will begin the healing process.

Whether there is a specific reason or several misunderstandings that lead to the end of a friendship or relationship, compassion, forgiveness, and grace can heal a wound that runs deep. We may never know why the other person moved on, but we can take responsibility for our pain and fill the space with love. When we let go, more love can enter.

Once you move forward, you will feel an immense sense of peace and spaciousness, ready to be filled with something lovely. Letting go always creates that beautiful void where what is longing to grow has the space it finally needs to evolve. I learned that to forgive does not always mean to restore. Sometimes forgiving means releasing and letting go completely or just for a time in order to allow healing to occur.

The healing that comes after the resolve to surrender to the process of forgiving is powerful. It can be overwhelming after feeling an emotion so intense as anger and resentment to experience peace, as negative emotions dissolve into a calm sensation that everything will be okay.

The most important lesson in forgiveness is the peace it provides. Whether letting go completely or restoring a relationship from a healed place, forgiveness offers peace of mind and clarity. There is a lightness that can only be felt once the weight of resentment, hurt, and bitterness is lifted. Forgiveness heals and restores the lightness and replaces the weight with immense peace.

It is a way to say,
"Peace be with you,
peace be with me."

"When you learn, teach.
When you get, give."

—MAYA ANGELOU

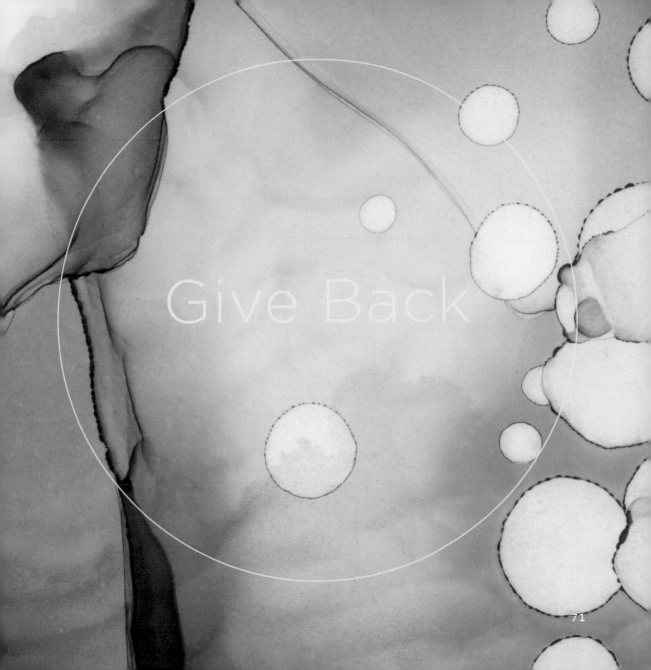

Give Back

When we give, we feel joy. The joy is even more full when we give back to a cause or a person that means a lot to us. Giving reminds us that there is always someone or some place to which we can extend love and help. Generosity is rooted in kindness and we can all be more kind to each other.

Each of us has been helped in some form, and the ability to give back creates a positive cache of energy, especially when it is personal.

We cultivate empathy when we can extend help to areas where we have been helped because of our deep understanding of a situation.

Giving comes in many forms. We can give gifts, money, kind words, and our time. You don't have to be rich to give back. When we give, our hearts become fuller. Giving from an open heart is as much a gift for the giver as it is for the receiver. To know that we are doing something for another person fills us with a sense of altruism.

I have a friend who is the epitome of giving back. She is constantly helping her neighbors and friends. I commented on how I was impressed by her selflessness and she replied, "The best thing to do when you are caught up in your own problems is to do something for others, get outside of yourself. It will change your perspective on whatever is going on in your own life."

It's so true that doing something for others redirects energy and expands perception. It is hard to stay in your head with your own issues when you are in service to others.

My friend is a shining example; she glows brightly because her heart is continually expanding by just doing what comes naturally to her: helping others.

It is easy to get caught up in our own problems and not notice the needs that are all around us. When you feel down or hopeless, look for a place to give.

By extending your heart towards another person, your energy will change, and your focus will shift outside of yourself and help you gain perspective.

If you are wondering where you can give back. I encourage you to think back to a time when someone helped you through a hard time or reflect on a cause that is important to you. With this memory, notice the feeling you had when you received help or how you feel when the cause that you care deeply about benefits. When we give with purpose, we feel it deeply. The connection to past pain and relief will be memorable and expansive. When our hearts expand, we shine brighter.

I remember volunteering with my sister to make food baskets at Thanksgiving with our youth group. The next day, our doorbell rang and there was one of the food baskets we had made, including the encouraging note we had decorated. Several years later, my husband asked me to help him to deliver food baskets in San Diego during the Thanksgiving holiday. I was happy to join him, remembering the gratitude I felt years ago.

GIVING BACK

Giving back is like that—you never know the ripple effect it creates. When you can recall a moment of deep gratitude and are able to create that same feeling for another being, it radiates from within.

If you're still not sure where to start, here are some suggestions:

- Think of a cause that means something to you. It can be a non-profit, animals, the arts—anything that has meaning for you.

- Recall a time when someone went out of his or her way to do something nice for you.

- Reach out to a friend who may be going through a difficult time.

- Search online for local volunteer opportunities.

There are so many needs all around us. We just have to know where to find them. Our friends and family are a great place to begin. When we start to look outside of ourselves, we notice the needs around us and become more attuned to where we can give.

Giving is one of the quickest ways to feel abundant. When we give of our time, gifts, or talents, we notice just how abundant we really are. Even if you feel extremely scarce you have something to give. All gifts don't have to be material possessions; remember that your time and effort are just as appreciated as a monetary gift.

The act of generosity will actually bring abundance into your life. When you are generous, you are telling the universe,

"Thank you for the good in my life,
I feel blessed and want to share the
goodness you have provided."

This is high vibrational thinking. The energy we emit, comes back to us.

Next time you are feeling overwhelmed or scarce, I challenge you to take a moment to find a need outside of yourself. Extend some time, money, or effort and change the energy of your day.

Giving is the perfect way
to offer gratitude to the universe
for all the good that is in your life
and bring hope to where it is
desperately needed.

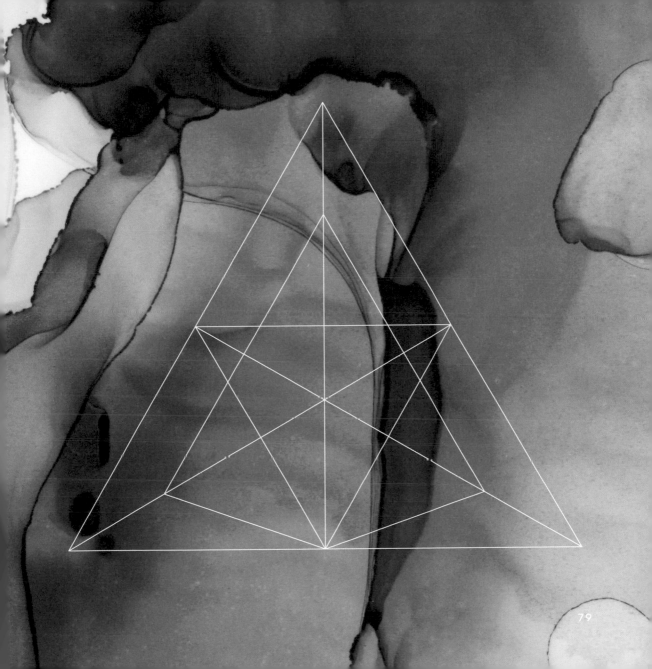

79

"There is a stubbornness about me that never can bear to be frightened at the will of others. My courage always rises at every attempt to intimidate me."

—JANE AUSTEN, *PRIDE AND PREJUDICE*

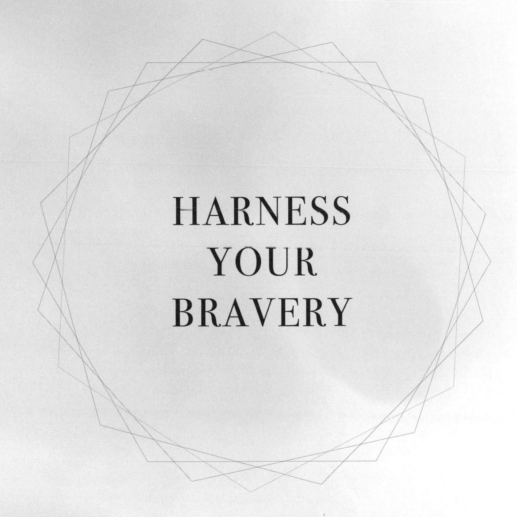

HARNESS
YOUR
BRAVERY

Courage requires confidence and listening to your heart. You have to believe in your decisions and trust your intuition in order to harness your bravery. You won't know what's waiting on the other side of the decision until you move forward. When you take a step into the unknown, courage invites trust to help you know that everything will be okay.

Learning to harness your bravery is one of the most rewarding lessons. When we learn to move past fear and into the unknown with trust, we are able to actualize our dreams by going after what we truly desire, even if we don't know all the answers right away. In the end, we will feel more confident and have greater trust in our intuition.

Trusting our intuition feeds our souls by helping us understand that we are brave and can do hard things.

My journey into bravery began years ago when I was on a trip to Costa Rica. "I'm going to give you a word; Brave," my intuitive painting teacher said as we were wrapping up our session. "But, I'm not brave," I replied with tears in my eyes. She reached over, grabbed my hand and said, "You are brave. We are all brave." I left her studio feeling excited to harness the bravery that she saw in me.

When I returned home, I decided to quit the job that had been my security for five years. I had been wanting to leave but was so afraid of the unknown.

Even when I reasoned why I needed to stay with the part of me that wanted to quit, my soul continued to feel uneasy. The answer was crystal clear, but my fear had been taking over.

Fear is very good at lying and making a case for all the tall tales it provides. It is so good that we can begin to believe that fear speaks the truth. When we listen to fear, we muffle intuition, but we don't silence it. It's that moment of insight when you know that it is essential to move forward rather than stay put. Even when moving forward is the only viable option, you can feel frozen in time, unable to transcend your doubts.

Bravery takes place when we decide to act. When we take a leap, it feels like a weight is being lifted. You will feel lighter and more alive. The unknown is ahead of you, but once you make a decision that is meant to be, bravery propels you forward. Aligning with your soul creates space for what is meant to be to enter your life next.

Bravery's call usually comes from a place deep within, and some examples of putting it into action are to quit your job, end a bad relationship, start your own business, get on stage, have that important conversation, fall in love, or many other things that seem scary.

We can all do hard things; it's a fact of life.

Just think about where you are now and what you have gone through to get here. You have overcome obstacles and are brave! Even with this truth, there are times when bravery seems to have disappeared. But remember, bravery is always with you.

Here are three tips to harness your bravery and overcome your next obstacle. These tips are meant to help you tap into your innate courage.

1. Reframe limiting beliefs and fear-based thoughts.

Fear has a tendency to swoop in and say a variety of things to prevent us moving forward. Negative thoughts are limiting beliefs that we have created, and they can be reframed with practice. When you notice these thoughts creeping in, reframe them with an empowering thought.

This exercise is powerful because when we get stuck in our heads it helps to get the thoughts out on paper. Instead of allowing the thoughts to endlessly circulate, write them out and empower yourself by reframing the thoughts that don't serve you.

2. Create an action plan.

Fear can be a motivator or a paralyzer. Brave people are *afraid but active.* Inaction can create complacency and it is easy to get stuck and give up. Creating an action plan is a great way to tackle this obstacle. This can be as simple as writing out everything you need to do to move forward, or you can even create a detailed plan.

Once you make a list of all the things you need to do, choose just one thing that you can do in the next forty-eight hours to get the ball rolling. Even if it is a baby step, it is forward motion. Action will create momentum towards your goal and is one of the most effective tools of bravery. Think of a hiker, who puts one foot in front of the other, slowly making his or her way to the top of a mountain.

Keep moving. Hire a coach or enlist a friend to hold you accountable. You do not have to embark on this journey alone.

3. Embrace ambiguity.

Bravery = adventure, and it isn't an adventure if we know what is around every corner. There are supposed to be unknown twists and turns—this is when growth and awe occur. Think about a time when you didn't know what to expect and how, in the end, everything turned out alright. Sometimes things can be better than expected. But if we hold on to the need to know, we create an expectation and can block the thing happening that is trying to occur.

Letting go is key, and one of the greatest tools to help you let go is meditation.

Taking the time to breathe into the anxiety that ambiguity creates can help dissipate its power. Stillness is also a space in which you can hear your soul speak. When we get inside our heads, our thoughts can be overpowering. Taking the time to stop, breathe, and reset is an effective way to release the grip of control and find the flow of your soul.

Trust that everything will all be revealed in due time and enjoy the ride. Bravery grows in ambiguity and you will emerge with a better story and sense of self if you let things fall as they intend to.

Working through fear by taking action and embracing the unknown is courageous and rewarding.

On the other side of our fear is strength and the actualizing of our desires. Your bravery is always available to you to harness. You are meant to do amazing things and your greatest tools are within you.

CULTIVATE

BRAVERY

A good exercise for reframing your thoughts is to make a list with two columns. On the left-hand side, list your limiting beliefs and fear-based thoughts; on the right-hand side, reframe each thought into an empowering one. When you find yourself stuck in negative thought patterns, you can access this list to reframe and reset. A few examples would look like:

- I can't seem to find the time to go after what I really want.

- I can't start my business because I don't know where to begin and it's been done before.

- This is important to me and I will spend some time tomorrow morning doing research instead of looking at my phone to help me move closer to my goal.

- I am capable of learning new things and will learn how to start my business. People need what I have to offer and my perspective is valuable.

"Our aspirations are
our possibilities."

—SAMUEL JOHNSON

IDENTIFY YOUR INTENTIONS

Setting intentions is a way to create soulful momentum in your life. Each of us have desires, and when they are clearly defined we can take steps to make them a reality. Being able to identify what we want is important, but taking it a step further and identifying why we want what we want creates momentum for action.

Intentions are goals with soul; they help you dig deep into why you want to do what you set out to do. I ask clients these two questions when we begin to work together: "What do you want?" and "How do you want your life to look and feel?" We then set an intention for our time together, and these intentions become a goal post for each week, month, or year that we work together.

I learned the power of intentions after noticing the many times I have set goals, only to watch them go undone or not even get started on them. When I started focusing on why I wanted to do these things and the feelings that coincided with the reasons, I was able to better equip myself for success.

I have been setting monthly intentions for years. It is amazing to look back at the intentions that I have set over the past several years and what has transpired from them. Some took a few months to come to fruition, while others were redirected into something greater than I could have imagined.

Focus and clarity have been key to manifesting what I desire. When I decided to start my business, I didn't have a clear idea about what that meant, but I knew I wanted to work for myself. Each month I tried to become clearer about what this business looked like. I wrote down: "I want to start a business where I help women get through difficult changes in their lives and grow spiritually." When I was clear on my intention and why I wanted to start a business, everything started to fall into place.

What we pay attention to grows.

With an intention, there is clarity; with clarity comes focus; with focus, actions can be taken and results then occur. Intentions are goals with soul because it takes more than writing a to-do list to achieve them. Setting an intention requires listening to your soul and paying attention to what and why you actually want to do something.

As your path continues to reveal itself to you, answers will come. When you have moments of doubt, return to your intention and look for ways in which you can take action in that moment instead of sitting in the confusion and fear.

Identifying intentions will help you get clear on what you want, why you want it, and how you can make it happen.

If you want to create a monthly ritual to set intentions, here is a five-step process I have created that I use myself and share with my clients. I encourage you to take what resonates with you and create a ritual of your own.

I usually set intentions with the full moon. Some use the new moon, others love the first of the month, choose whatever works best for you and is the best reminder to set your intentions. Make sure you can give some time to focusing on what you want and why you want it.

1. **Meditate.**
Sit quietly and meditate on the coming month. Notice what has been transpiring in your life. Then sit with your breath and ask, "What do I want?" You can repeat this question or just ask it once. Allow the stillness and silence to bring answers to you.

2. **Write it down.**
Once you figure out what it is that you want, make a list of your intentions for the month. Focus on what you want to spend the next month creating, changing, manifesting, and focusing on. "I intend to _____" is a positive and powerful statement.

3. **Visualize.**
With each intention, visualize what the outcome looks like. See yourself in the situation that you desire. Notice what it feels like to see the outcome you want. Pay attention to what you see, hear, and feel during your visualization. This step helps create positive energy around the intention. This vision is always available to you and should be accessed when doubt or fear arise.

4. Release and let go.

In order to welcome growth into your life, something might have to be released. What are the things you need to release and let go of? What no longer serves you? Intend to let these things go, see them disappear into the sky until you can no longer visualize them. If it is something physical, throw it away or donate it.

5. Offer gratitude.

To seal the ritual, offer gratitude. Offer gratitude for your intention as if it is already happening or has arrived by thanking the universe for the goodness in your life. The universe is constantly listening to our deepest desires, and when we take a step towards actualizing them, it meets us where we are at.

When you identify what you want, how you want to feel and take the time to visualize it into existence, it is amazing what transpires. Our inner glow is nurtured because we are going after what is important to our souls. When we take time to tend to our desires, we create an energy for momentum and for the universe to meet us where we are at to help us along the way.

"The habit of writing
for my eye is good practice.
It loosens the ligaments."

—VIRGINIA WOOLF

Journaling

Have you ever felt trapped in your mind with thoughts and ideas swirling about that leave you unfocused and anxious? It is easy to get inside our heads, lost in our thoughts, and allow stress and anxiety to take over. There are so many reasons why we can get trapped inside our heads, and every day we are presented with various distractions, especially now with smartphones. We can retrieve information whenever we want, causing us to stay preoccupied and not in the present moment. There is a constant barrage of information coming our way and it can feel overwhelming to process it all.

Sometimes the information we take in leaves us feeling worse than before we consumed it. The same goes for interactions with people. There are times when we need to vent and get everything out that can potentially be bottled up and can lead to bitterness and resentment which dulls our glow. We need an outlet, a safe one, where we can let everything out without judgement or fear of criticism.

Journaling is essential for getting out of your head and transferring all your thoughts somewhere else.

I call this a brain dump. I have been journaling since I was a child; I remember telling my deepest, darkest secrets to my journal and feeling relieved that I was no longer bearing the great weight of my truth. Even now, when I feel my thoughts piling up, journaling is a perfect way for me to process and let go of the things that weigh me down.

A journal can be the first place we go to process our thoughts, especially if they keep us from focusing. Sometimes all we need to do is write them down and leave them there, but other times we might say the same things over and over as we deal with the emotions. There are occasions when I look through my journal and realize that it took me weeks and sometimes months to fully sort out certain issues.

We all want to be listened to and heard. It can be frustrating to speak to someone who is just waiting for his or her turn to respond or say, "Oh my goodness, I had that same thing happen…" and then continue with his or her story, leaving you mid-sentence, mid-thought, mid-process. With journaling, we can get everything out in one sitting. There is a cathartic element to spilling your feelings onto paper, even if it doesn't necessarily make sense.

Journaling does not have to be a formal writing experience; it can serve as a place to get everything out of your head, including lists and half sentences. We have so many thoughts that we recycle in our minds that it is helpful to get them out and process them so we can start thinking about something else and focus on what is truly important.

Answering questions helps start the process and is an intuitive way to approach journaling. Try asking the question and then allowing whatever needs to come out, appear on the page.

Self-Expression

Another effective way to journal is to begin your writing with a question. Here are a few questions you can ask yourself daily/weekly/monthly:

- How am I doing today?

- What have I done today to create momentum towards living the life I desire?

- What did I do today that I am most proud of?

- How am I supporting my values each day?

- What do I want to happen in this situation and why?

- Where did I face challenges today and how did they affect me?

- Who or what surprised me this week?

I like to think of this as a dialogue with the soul, because when we quiet our minds, our souls can speak. Just allow the words to flow and don't worry about whether they make sense.

Write without editing—journaling is not about perfection, it is about processing and catharsis. You can go back and read what you were thinking in the exact way that you were thinking it. When we write freely, we let go and release the thoughts, fears, anxieties, and issues that take up precious space in our minds.

When you find a practice that works for you, it will feel therapeutic to let go of the day's thoughts and troubles.

Anne Frank lovingly called her diary Kitty, because it was like a friend to her, one who always listened without interruption. Feeling heard is so important, and when we can get all of our thoughts and frustrations out in one sitting, it's such a relief.

Release stress and anxiety by getting everything out of your head and onto paper. Journaling has positive benefits for your well-being and will help you find clarity and feel heard. Give yourself a gift of self-care by taking the time to journal.

When you sort through your thoughts, you can access your inner glow that may have been dimmed by the overwhelming need to process everything that is in your head.

"Far away there in the sunshine
are my highest aspirations.
I may not reach them, but I can
look up and see their beauty,
believe in them, and try
to follow where they lead."

—LOUISA MAY ALCOTT

Know Your Purpose

Purpose can feel like a loaded word. Knowing why you are here and what you're supposed to be doing with your life can be daunting if you don't know where to start. Each of us has a gift that we are here to give. Once we realize our gifts, we can then bring them forth into the world. Our soul knows our purpose, but it is our mind that sometimes gets in the way of fully understanding what we are here to do. Overthinking such a big question like "What is my purpose?" can create anxiety and self-doubt.

Our purpose doesn't always equate to the way we bring in money but it definitely gives us a sense of accomplishment. Our jobs can provide a sense of purpose and, for some of us, fulfill our purpose. However, not all of us can make a living in our purpose, but we must put ourselves in the position to exercise it, because when we aren't living in our purpose life doesn't seem fulfilling.

When clients come to me because they want to switch careers, it is most always because they want to find a sense of purpose and fulfillment. Being able to seek change where there is comfort and security is courageous. The very first thing we work on is gaining clarity about what their hopes and desires are, in order to identify purpose.

Asking "why" is crucial to knowing our purpose, because it is always the driver behind why we need or want to do something. Our talents and desires are unique to each of us; we come equipped with abilities and longings to learn certain things. When we take our talents and desires and put them into action it feels amazing. This is the feeling of knowing and living in your purpose.

Of course, there is work involved, and sometimes it's hard work. Identifying and then acting on purpose is fulfilling. Sometimes trials and pain illuminate our purpose because we want to help others who are going through similar painful experiences; we become a wounded healer.

There are many people who derive a sense of purpose after going through a hard situation. Not wanting their pain to be in vain, their resilient spirits help them to rise from the ashes. By sharing their stories, they let others know that they are not alone, that there is hope and a light at the end of the tunnel.

In some cases, there is a cause that resonates so deeply that it becomes a mission in life to work, advocate, or donate to the cause. When we feel connected to something at a deep, visceral level, it is hard to ignore. This is a soul connection and a calling to step up and act.

When I decided to start my business, I knew that I wanted to help people who were going through difficult changes. I wish I had known about life coaching when I was navigating career changes and ending a bad relationship, because I would have hired one in a heartbeat! All the pain that I felt during that transition was a driver for me to learn how to help people embrace change proactively.

The more you step in the direction of your purpose, the more things will fall into place.

CULTIVATE

Purpose

I have had the honor of watching several women identify their purpose and then courageously take steps towards living it. There are so many variations of purpose out there and each of us has a specific calling deep within our souls. To know your purpose, it is important to take the time to think about and answer some essential questions. Here are a few questions you can ask yourself:

- What did I like to do when I was a child? Was there an activity that I always found myself doing or thinking about doing?

- What do people consistently come to me for?

- What am I doing when I am feeling my best?

- What drives me and why?

It won't always be easy, but knowing that you are moving towards your purpose is rewarding. Every time you feel like stepping away in fear or doubt, keep pushing forward and working towards your goal. Things will fall into place as you continue to move forward. It takes time, but trust that it is happening.

When you take the time to answer the questions provided and explore your "why," you can begin to take action towards living your purpose. Take the clarity that you found and make a list of what you can do to create momentum, then break down the list into manageable action steps. With each step, you will feel energized because your actions will create a life of purpose.

Finding out what our souls are here to do feels rewarding.

We are meant to live a life of fulfillment and happiness.

Taking soulful action lights us up and when we live with purpose, we glow brighter than ever before.

111

"When I let go of what I am,
I become what I might be. When
I let go of what I have, I receive
what I need."

—TAO TE CHING

LET GO

When things fall apart, it can be hard to find the incentive to get back up to find the space to start over or create something new. Days can seem to drag and putting one foot in front of the other can seem like a huge feat. Sometimes, it can feel as if you are stuck and doomed to live in a cycle of disappointment.

It is easy to want to hold on to the idea of how we think things should be. When we try to rationalize why things fall apart or something doesn't make sense, there is a need to understand and sometimes to exert control. The need to control is intoxicating because we then feel in charge of our life and able to steer its direction.

However, sometimes we just need to let go and release our grip on the situation.

In 2008, the bank I worked for was bought by a bigger bank and the market started its infamous decline. My job went from helping people save for their dreams to dealing with a new mega-corporation's expectations and hearing tragic stories of people losing their homes and life savings. My job became extremely stressful and I wasn't growing professionally. I knew that it was time to go, but I feared what would be next.

I was anxious about leaving because the job provided security, but the longer I stayed, the more miserable I became. I didn't know how to move forward, but I also knew that I couldn't live that way much longer. After I decided to let go of control, I was able to find answers to what was next and then take action to move forward.

After we let go, it is important to take some time to allow the answer to arrive. The need for control will make us feel like we need to do something immediately, but that is not truly letting go.

Taking time to search for answers helps us sort through the disappointment and heal from the pain and fear of letting go. Figuring out action steps can help bring your mind out of the fog, but make sure you give yourself time to process the disappointment. If it is time to move on, it's okay to mourn the loss. Allow the healing to occur and take an active role by looking forward to creating something new when the time is right.

Be honest with yourself and take time to write out your responses to the questions on the next page. After you answer the questions, look to see if anything sticks out. Are there common themes, new revelations, or is the answer clear and did the writing exercise solidify your intuition? Sit with your answers, meditate on the next steps, and recognize any closure that needs to take place.

Perhaps the most important thing to note is the last question. If where you are now does not help you get to where you want to be, then the answer is clear: getting clear on what you want to do can ease the pain of ending something that is not meant to be.

When things end, it is important to get back up, even if it takes some time. Making daily efforts to try again seems difficult at first, but after a while the practice of "doing" creates the momentum needed to move forward.

In order to allow growth to take place, movement is necessary.

CULTIVATE
LETTING GO

Some important questions to ask when there
is something that may feel like it is falling apart are:

1. What isn't working?

2. Is there something I can change to make it work?

3. If I let go and move on from this, what are my next actions?

4. What do I want to be working towards?

When life gives us a "no," it creates space for expansion. This is a place for possibility and dreaming. The opposite of expansion is contracting. If contracting is happening, it holds on to pain and disappointment. Stagnation can occur and often resentment too. Imagine a fist releasing its grasp—notice how the hand expands as it lets go of its tight hold.

Resistance blocks flow from occurring in our lives. When we resist, what is meant to leave stays and what is meant to come is blocked. When you are faced with letting go, notice any areas where you may feel resistance. What is keeping you stuck? Visualize removing that block and letting the good flow in and the bad flow out. Be open. Wonderful things are on their way.

Release and expand; these are the actions most beneficial for moving on.

Let what needs to fall down, fall. Whatever is falling apart does not need to be a curse. Look to see the blessing in disguise.

There is something waiting for this to end in order to have the space it needs to enter your life.

Let go and receive whatever may come with open arms, mind, and heart. Replace resistance with cooperation. Momentum can aid in cooperation, and soon moving forward will feel exciting and new beginnings will emerge. All you have to do is be honest with yourself, find clarity, and start moving forward, step by step. In time, the space will be filled with something new.

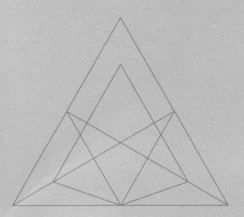

"Meditate. Live purely. Be quiet. Do your work with mastery. Like the moon, come out from behind the clouds! Shine."

—BUDDHA

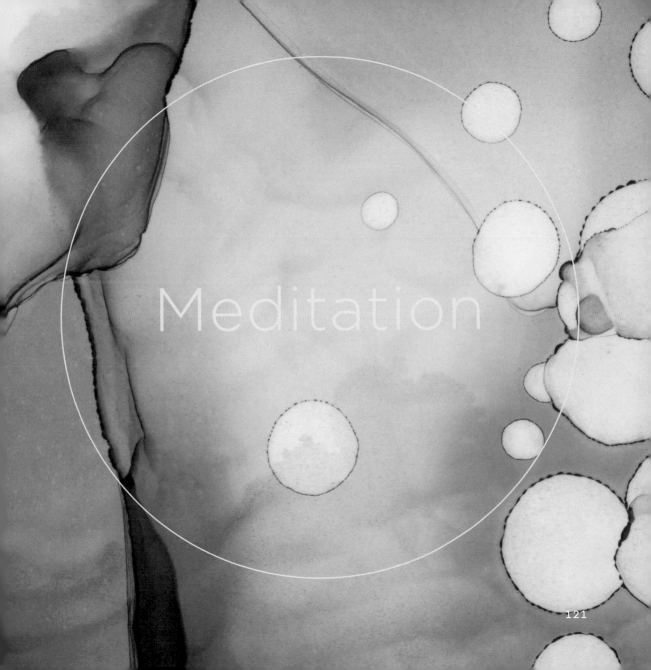

Meditation

Do you ever feel like your mind goes a mile a minute? At any time of the day, do you have at least three things going through your head? When we are constantly trying to figure out, fix, plan, or contemplate something, we are not living in the present moment.

I used to pride myself on my brain's capacity to multi-task, until I realized that I was actually less effective in the various tasks because I wasn't giving each one the full attention it needed. This whirlwind of activity also caused stress and anxiety when I couldn't figure things out or when my plans didn't go as expected. I knew something needed to change, and this is when I started to recognize the power of stillness in the form of prayer, meditation, and visualization.

Meditation brings you back to your breath and soul. Just five minutes can shift your energy and quiet any anxiety and mind chatter. Stillness offers the time to check in, calm down, and quiet fear's voice. It is amazing that just five minutes can calm the endless loop of chatter, anxiety, and thoughts.

True vibrancy comes from within—the light in our eyes, the radiance in a smile, the glow on our skin are all manifestations of how we take care of ourselves inwardly. Spiritual health is just as important as physical health. We can improve our health by taking some time each day to find stillness. Learning to breathe in the stillness and breathe out chaos invites calm.

By beginning to practice meditation you will notice that your mind can calm even deeper. Learning how to still your mind and just allow your breath to course through you without the interruption of words is powerful.

At first, meditation can be difficult, especially if you believe that you need to get your mind completely still and that you will have reached mastery once you can sit without a single thought or word entering your brain. But this is not true, as meditation provides the space and time for stillness. Thoughts will come and go while you sit, but the key is to let them go.

Meditation teaches that thoughts will never cease, but attachment can dissipate with practice.

Attachment to outcomes and expectations is where a lot of pain is rooted. There are a myriad of possible "what ifs" and "maybes," but the important thing is to come back to the present moment. Meditation is a tool that brings presence into each day.

You can enhance your practice by visualizing the things that you want and the emotions you want to feel.

If something is very important to you, spend some time seeing it as if it is already happening. This practice will exercise your trust in the universe and bring a sense of peace. When you are able to see and feel what you have prayed for and meditated on, the need to control falls away and your mind welcomes whatever is meant to happen in its own time.

Visualization releases the vibrational energy into the universe, saying, "I am ready to receive."

Meditation is not the absence of thought, it is connecting with your breath and finding the space for stillness. There are many ways to meditate. Guided meditation is a favorite place to begin for those of us who need help to quiet our own thoughts. By hearing someone speak, it can help us get out of our heads and relax. Some people receive mantras and focus on them while meditating. Others just sit in silence noticing their thoughts as they arise and allowing them to melt away.

Meditation is an act of letting go.

With each lesson of surrender, our souls are opening even more in a new expansiveness. Possibilities are endless, and going with the flow, although still difficult at times, has proved to be the best way to cultivate stillness and presence in our lives.

This is a practice that gets easier the more you do it. At first, the most important thing will be to learn how to become still. This lesson alone is extremely beneficial.

Mindfulness

When you find yourself looking for answers, meditation can be a great tool. When we quiet the conscious mind, we can sift through all the ideas and thoughts in our subconscious. Here are a few steps to help:

1. Try sitting still. Close your eyes and begin to feel yourself relax from your toes to the top of your head. Do this in sections: feel your feet relax, then your legs, then your abdomen, your throat, face, and finally your entire body.

2. Let your breath be your guide. Take a deep breath in through your nose, and out through your nose. Count to ten, using the breath for each count: one – breathe in, two – breathe out, etc.

3. Ask your question, wait for the answer, breathing in and out as you do so.

4. If a thought emerges, notice it, acknowledge it, and send it on its way—don't stop and dwell, just let it go and continue breathing.

In time, you will notice answers and ideas pop up. Stillness gives them room to emerge.

Sometimes the most important place to be is nowhere.

One of the benefits of meditation is quieting the mind and giving space to the things that needs to be dealt with. This space allows calm to occur. When we can learn to calm our anxiety with breath our entire body benefits. We get so busy that it is easy to stuff down our thoughts, neglect self-care, and dismiss emotions. In stillness, we can find the answers we seek, connect with our mind and body, and allow emotions to flow so we can be more present.

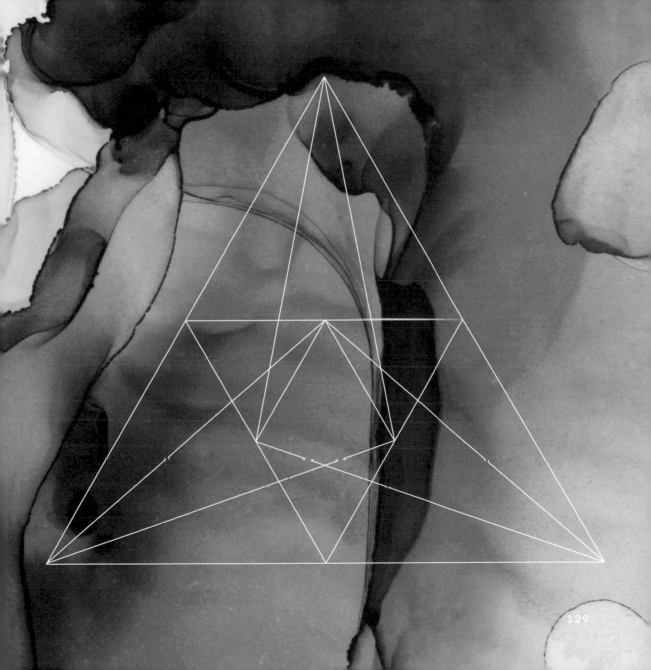

129

"The first wealth is health."

—RALPH WALDO EMERSON

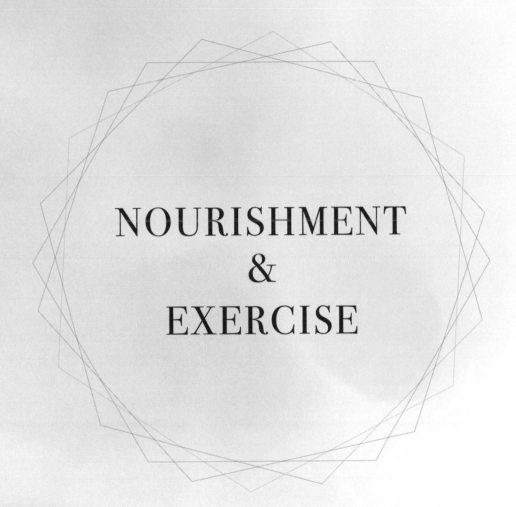

NOURISHMENT
&
EXERCISE

t is essential to take care of our bodies in order to live our most vibrant lives. What we eat and do with our bodies plays a huge part in our inner glow.

What we put into our bodies, we emit physically, and the energy we put out, such as exercise, can help us maintain and restore our glow.

As we age, it becomes more apparent that how we take care of ourselves shows. Eating well and exercising are essential to not only taking care of our bodies but also our minds and spirits.

The foods we eat carry energy. Most of what we eat is or once was living, and because of this, food carries its own vibrational frequency. When we eat things that are at a higher vibrational frequency, we raise our vibration. For instance, greens are amazing at keeping us healthy because they are living when they are cut and so move easily through our digestive system. Think about how you feel when you eat processed foods—although they taste good, they don't necessarily move through our systems as efficiently.

Even meat that is raised well and sustainably carries with it a higher vibration than meat that is overly produced, full of antibiotics and hormones, because of the conditions in which they were raised. If we do our best to choose food that is well taken care of, locally produced, and free of processing, we will feed our bodies with the best available options.

If these types of foods aren't always available, try to choose the best possible item to eat instead. When you go to a grocery store, shop on the perimeters where all the fresh foods are—the center aisles tend to be where we find the processed foods. Farmers' markets are also a wonderful place to get fresh foods, and you can speak to local farmers about how to incorporate their fruits and veggies into your recipes and diets.

Road trips are usually the hardest for me when it comes to feeding my body the best possible option. I used to drive six hours a day for my job in an area that was mainly agricultural, however, my eating options were restricted to fast-food chains. I had to consciously find places where I could eat foods that would keep my energy high, alert, and keep me feeling well. Restaurants have introduced healthier options to their menus since more people are becoming aware of how important nutrition is and want to have such options available.

At home, meal prep can be an effective way to ensure you are eating well because it helps you prepare nutritious meals ahead of time, so you have a delicious meal ready for when you are hungry. It also helps you create more mindful eating habits and steer you away from eating non-nutritious food items that may be easily accessible. Incorporating smoothies is another quick and easy way to add more greens into your diet. There are several diets you can follow that claim health benefits, but make sure you do the research before embarking on them to determine if they are the best choice for you.

In addition to eating well, movement is very important for keeping our minds, bodies, and souls at their best.

A sedentary lifestyle attributes to myriad health issues, and something as simple as going outside to take a walk can lower anxiety and depression.

There are so many ways to incorporate movement into your life. Getting outside is easy and accessible. There are also several different fitness classes you can try, including yoga, Pilates, and strength training, so go to a few and see if you can find one that you enjoy. Joining a class can also help to create a sense of community and accountability, which can make movement more enjoyable.

A few years ago, I trained for twelve weeks to run the Cherry Blossom ten-miler in Washington, D.C. During my training I had shin splints, foot pain, and sore muscles. I had rarely pushed myself that far before physically and I felt every milestone. I didn't let the discomfort keep me from reaching my goal, though.

One of the most important changes that I made to get through the training was to surround myself with other runners. My running friends were encouraging and helpful with advice and tips on training and gear. Mentally, I began seeing workouts, food, and drink in a different light. I wanted to be successful in attaining my goal, but not obsessive. I worked on balance and meditated on the result.

I think about muscles and how they have to tear and break down in order to grow. In the last few minutes of the race, I broke down, but that was because I was growing. Doing hard things helps us grow. I wanted to quit, but I persisted. I felt a sense of accomplishment and pride as I made it over the finish line.

Creating a self-care ritual around food and exercise will help to create healthy habits and keep you glowing your brightest!

It can be hard to carve out some time for yourself and not feel like you are leaving a bunch of things to keep piling up.

The thing is, if you aren't taking care of yourself you won't have the energy to do the things that you need to do. When we have many things and people to take care of, we need to make sure we prioritize our care first and foremost, so we can show up for those who need us.

To create a self-care ritual, come up with a list of non-negotiables, the things that you must do to feel your best. The list can be as short or as long as you need it to be. For instance, my non-negotiables are meditation, green smoothie, and a walk. I need those three things every day to feel my best.

MINDFUL HABITS

If it is hard to think of your non-negotiables, to think about what you absolutely need, then ask yourself:

- If I had thirty minutes to myself every morning and evening, what would I want to do?

- How can I better take care of myself?

- What are my mind, body, and soul craving?

Once you come up with your non-negotiable list, find a time each day to make sure they happen. They can be incorporated into your morning routine or throughout the day.

The key is to make sure that you are getting what you need to take care of yourself.

Try this for a week and notice any changes that occur. When we take time to care for ourselves, we show up better, glow brighter and most importantly, we feel better.

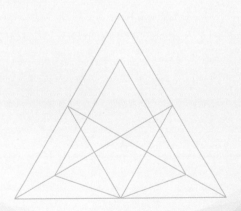

"We do not need magic to change the world, we carry all the power we need inside ourselves already: We have the power to imagine better."

—J.K. ROWLING

OWN YOUR POWER

Y ou are more powerful than you give yourself credit for. It's true! We have the power to influence people with our actions, emotions, and words. When we get honest with ourselves to live and speak our truth, we connect to our power. In this truth, we have the capacity to create our destiny.

The problem is, many of us don't recognize that we possess this inner power and in turn own it.

When we step into our power, our inner glow shines brightly, and we can feel its effects throughout our entire being.

We can manifest things into our lives, create change, and make a difference when we own our unique power.

When we decide to step into our power, we hold ourselves differently, we believe the best of ourselves and others, we create necessary changes with confidence and grace because we know we can. Second-guessing and doubt take a back seat to action and confidence. Life can harden or soften us with everything that comes our way. Resilience keeps us going and helps us tap into our inner strength time and again.

A resilient spirit is powerful. To be able to get up after a hardship takes strength and the trust that everything can and will be better than the current situation. Inner power breeds trust and confidence, and vice versa. You cannot live riddled with doubt and feel powerful. The key is to boost confidence and learn how to trust yourself. When you can do these two things, recognizing and owning your power becomes easy.

One of the topics that consistently comes up in coaching is finding the confidence for a job interview, salary negotiation, and in personal affairs. Many of my clients don't want to apply for a job that they don't feel qualified for, believing that it is a waste of time. My advice has always been that if you're truly interested in the job, apply anyway. You never know who is applying and what their qualifications are. If you are honest about your experience and willing to learn, you can show up confident without anything to hide.

Asserting oneself can make us feel uneasy, because we don't want to rock the boat. We end up stepping aside to allow someone else to shine and get that job, and risk not getting what we really want. There have been plenty of people who have applied for jobs that they aren't one-hundred percent qualified for and ended up getting the job. I know, because it has happened to me and several of my clients.

> # They key is to be confident that you can learn and confident that this is the direction in which you want to go. Confidence comes with clarity.

When we can clearly define what we want, we can visualize the outcome and communicate with confidence. Clarity is the super power when it comes to negotiations and communication. A well thought-out argument is more likely to be heard. When we can paint a clear picture or scenario of what and why we want something, we can get the point across with ease.

I remember when I wanted to negotiate my salary; I felt fear and doubt rising inside of me, thwarting my confidence and telling me several reasons why it would not happen. I chose to sit in that painful place for a moment but I knew that I was the only one who could be my own champion. I went back and forth on approaching my boss, and after careful planning, I took the leap and approached him with my proposal.

I had numbers to back up my performance, customer reviews, and a figure in my head that I wanted. I had done my research on comparable salaries and wanted to feel valued and appreciated. In fact, after all my careful planning, I realized that the underlying reason for my request was because I wanted to feel valued.

This can be said in personal affairs, too. We all want to be seen and heard, and, most of all, valued. Confidence in communication does not need to be paired with arrogance, but it is better partnered with clarity.

When we communicate with confidence, we can be seen as more vibrant, attractive, intelligent, and calm.

Whether you are going in for an interview, negotiating a salary, or having a hard discussion with a loved one, taking the time to find clarity and confidence first will help ease the discomfort.

CULTIVATE

CONFIDENCE

So how to boost confidence? Here are a few steps to muster courage, grow your confidence quotient and communicate your value with clarity:

1. Make a list of what you want and why. (Note: the "why" is very important.)

2. Ask ten people what they believe your top three qualities/attributes are. Notice any commonalities. (Trust me, we all sell ourselves short and this is a way to find out how others view us and boost confidence.)

3. Back yourself up with examples, numbers, hard facts, and any information you need to show them you did your homework and know your stuff!

4. Visualize and breathe; close your eyes and see yourself negotiating, discussing, and receiving. Breathe into this feeling. Find your calm and replace the anxious thoughts with confident ones.

5. Power pose; if you don't know what I mean, watch Amy Cuddy's TED Talk, which has helped many people muster up courage right before their big talks, performances, negotiations.

Replace anxiety with anticipatory excitement. You are your own champion and we all want our superheroes to stand tall with confidence. Find yours within and embrace the bravery that lies inside.

You are powerful, and with confidence you can own your power and glow brighter than ever before.

"Find ecstasy in life;
the mere sense of living
is joy enough."

—EMILY DICKINSON

Prioritize
Joy

Joy is one of the most desirable emotions, and many of us would like more of it in our lives. We all want to be happy, and at times, it can feel as though joy is elusive, but we can always choose joy. When we feel down or find ourselves deep in negative thoughts, we can decide to change the energy of what we are feeling. Choosing joy does not mean that happiness is a constant state. It means that when joy is the hardest to feel, we can work on choosing it to strengthen emotional resilience.

Going through hard things makes joy even greater.

Eventually all things come to an end, including bad experiences. In fact, knowing sadness helps us to know joy even better. On the other side of pain is relief, and in that relief joy emerges. Instead of resisting any experience, go through it.

Resistance only breeds more pain. Feel what needs to be felt, and if it is particularly hard, give yourself grace and remind yourself that the pain is temporary.

There are many rewarding things that require hard work and effort. Think about Olympic athletes standing on the podium to receive their medal. Their faces are filled with joy, pride, and relief. The road towards that medal was paved with practice, pain, and difficulty. All the years of training led them to this moment of immense happiness.

Not all of us are Olympic athletes, but we do always have access to happiness and the feelings it invokes. To access what joy feels like, I try to remember times when I felt this emotion. When I visualize what this would look like, I think about those moments when my face scrunches up because a smile just isn't enough to express how happy I feel. I call these "heart smiles," and I have been known to use the expression "you/it made my heart smile" because these moments are when I feel joy so deeply. People, experiences, nature, and certain memories are things that bring so much joy, my heart bursts with happiness. The great thing is that feeling is always available to me and I can recall these moments, especially during hard times.

The months leading up to my wedding were particularly difficult. I was stressed out, which left me in an anxious and tired state most of the time. There were so many moving parts and I wanted everything to be perfect. What was supposed to be a happy event started turning into a great stress. But deep down, I was excited and wanted to do my best to find the joy in those moments, despite how I was feeling. Joy became a priority.

To remember what joy feels like, remember a time when you felt immense happiness, and deliberately try to tap into that sensation whenever you feel negative thoughts and emotions welling up. At first it can be difficult because it is easy to stay in low emotions, but as you continue this practice, joy will become easier to choose.

Joy lives deep within us and is ready to be recalled at a moment's notice.

Choosing to prioritize joy every day will change your outlook on life. Even during particularly stressful events, joy is nearby, waiting to be chosen. The beauty of recalling a joyful memory is that there is a sensation that accompanies it, so not only does your mind feel the switch, but your body can also feel joy. When we feel joy this strongly, we can't help but glow from the inside.

On the other hand, there are times when we just forget to prioritize joy because we get caught up in our routines and negative loops in the media or gossip. It is at these times that we need to catch ourselves and ask, "Is this something that is helping me prioritize joy or will it bring me down?"

It's important to take news and social media breaks, especially if you can feel the information bringing you down.

Digital detoxes also help to bring your mind to a calmer state and reconnect with stillness. You can choose to allow yourself to go into the spiral of bad news and social media comparison, or you can prioritize joy and remove yourself from the situation. The information will still be available if you decide to access it later.

Remember, this feeling of joy is available to you at any time. You can access it whenever you feel a negative emotional state. Just take a moment to practice this exercise during those times and the feelings of joy can arrive. The more we stop negative emotions from taking over and choose joy, the less frequently our brain will want to default to negativity.

This practice raises your vibration, and since like energy attracts like energy, higher vibrations will arrive. Joy's frequency will radiate your inner glow the more you decide that joy takes priority over lower emotions. You deserve to be happy and only you can make that happen.

Inner Joy

So, what can you do when you feel negativity creeping in?
Try this practice to help retrain the brain to find joy:

- Notice what is causing you to feel negative and step away.

- Identify one of the most joyful moments in your life, one where you felt like your heart would burst with happiness.

- Now REALLY feel it. Feel it in your heart, your mind, your skin, your gut…

- Sit with that feeling.

- Breathe in the positive vibes that memory provides.

- Notice the energy shift that occurs as you take a moment to choose joy.

"The more one judges,
the less one loves."

—HONORÉ DE BALZAC

QUIET
JUDGEMENTS

Judgements are part of our everyday lives. We wake up and judge what we should wear, eat, and even the weather. We judge others, ourselves, and how things are done. Not all judgements are bad; sometimes making a sound judgement keeps us from harm.

When judgements are negative, they can be addictive and help us create a story that keeps us from the truth. When we judge others, we are judging something inside ourselves. A judgement occurs when we become uncomfortable with something that hasn't been addressed or healed within us. For instance, if we judge someone's appearance, it is because there is something about our own appearance that we do not accept.

Judgements are defense mechanisms to protect a part of us that needs healing.

We place judgement on ourselves, on others, and we pass moral judgements when we don't agree with the way things are. The more stringent we are in our judgements, the more closed off we are to growth, and we dim our ability to shine from within.

When we live in a state of judgement, it leaves little to no room for seeing a different perspective or learning a new way of thinking. The driving forces behind negative judgements are judgement of self, fear, and the need to understand.

When we judge, it is usually an indication that there is something inside of us that needs attention or healing. We also judge what we don't understand or what is unfamiliar, which can sometimes cause fear in us. The first step to quieting judgements is to recognize where they are placed and then do the work to release them and heal the parts of us from where they stem.

Being aware of our judgements is the first step to noticing if there is a part of us that needs healing. This awareness will also illuminate whether we are creating a negative meaning behind something we don't understand or if we are just trying to create a meaning, so we can move on. Many times, we just need to create a meaning so we don't dwell on what we don't understand. However, when the judgement is based in negativity, we need to notice why and heal the part of us that is placing the judgement.

For years, I would judge people in relationships, always looking for the drama, thinking, "it can't be that good." But when I took a step back, I realized that, deep down, I craved a loving relationship and my judgements were a reflection of a longing that I had yet to fulfill and I hated feeling lonely.

> Only when I learned to quiet my judgement of other relationships was I able to see that my fear of being lonely was the real issue.

When I figured this out, I was able to do the hard work of dealing with my fear. If I had stayed in my cycle of judgements, I would never have healed my fear of loneliness and moved on from the pain of past relationships, or opened my heart to a new one.

Quieting judgements is difficult when there is a natural tendency to find fault. Recognizing what we don't accept about ourselves and facing our fears helps us quiet our inner critic. Getting real with our fear and recognizing our pain is a vulnerable thing to do, but in this space, healing is possible.

When we notice the things we don't like about ourselves and offer acceptance and love to them, we heal. Offering acceptance is an act of compassion. Embrace every part of yourself, and if you want to change something, change it, but don't keep the negative loop of self-deprecation running through your mind. Bring compassion where criticism is loudest, replacing it with love and understanding.

To quiet judgements, it is important to get honest and notice where you are being judgmental. What are the things that bother you, make you feel less than or things about yourself that you don't like?

Take the time to answer this honestly, and then ask, "Why do I feel the need to judge this?" Again, this is where honesty is a must. In order to heal, we have to allow our walls to come down and get real about why we are judging.

Then ask yourself, "What do I need to heal this judgement?" For instance, if you are judging someone's appearance and there is a part of you that you don't like, and it causes you to judge another, do the work to accept that part of yourself.

Since many judgements are based in fear, another exercise you can do is write down the judgement and then ask yourself, "What is the truth?" and then, "What can I do to offer love or compassion?" For instance, if you judge another person because he or she is different than you and you feel yourself avoiding them, you may have created a story to justify your judgements. However, if you ask yourself what the truth is, you will be able to find your own course of action to offer acceptance.

Finally, forgive yourself for judging. Release the negative energy around judgement by recognizing it, confronting it, healing it, and then forgiving it.

Forgiveness offers a release of attachment to the judgement.

From this place, we can learn to accept differences and ourselves more. When we heal our inner judge, forgiveness and acceptance replace fear and criticism.

SELF-AWARENESS

Here are a few examples on answering the questions, "What is the truth and what can I do to offer love and compassion":

- I don't understand them so I should take the time to learn more about them.

- They look different from me and this makes me uncomfortable, so I should try to accept their difference and see their beauty.

- I've heard things that I don't agree with, but I am not sure if that's even the truth, so I should do my own research by speaking with them directly.

"And even as it's affecting our health, sleep deprivation will also profoundly affect your creativity, your productivity, and your decision-making."

—ARIANNA HUFFINGTON

Restore
Your
Energy

Rest is extremely important, and in our hyper-connected world it seems that now, more than ever, it is more difficult to get our minds to settle down. For super-productive types, rest seems like a waste of time. The praise of being busy and the criticism of rest can keep us overstimulated and our calendars full.

Being busy does not necessarily mean being productive. One day I made a list and decided to prioritize it, and I realized that there were things that I was doing just to fill time. I never stopped to even think about them since I was "so busy." When I recognized this, I easily cut them out of my schedule and was able to rest with even more ease.

Rest does not only mean sleep, it also means taking breaks from productivity to restore energy. If we operate at a harried pace, we eventually burn out and are then forced to rest. It doesn't have to be this way.

By incorporating rest into each day, we can restore and maintain our energy more easily.

In rest, a stillness is created that can result in deeper peace.

In this state, we can hear our soul and give it what it needs. Releasing the need to get everything done and be constantly busy helps you focus your attention and create space for relaxation. Embrace rest by releasing the attachment to being busy.

There are always things that need to be done, but my challenge to you would be to look at your schedule, prioritize tasks, and see what you can cut away to make room for rest. Start small and let go of at least one thing. Slowly remove the excess from your life to create balance and peace.

One of the most important actions we do each day is sleep.

If we aren't getting enough sleep, everything suffers. I used to wear my insomnia like a badge of honor in college. I thought that working a few jobs, going to class, and staying up late to get my papers written was admirable. But in reality, I was doing more harm than good by not taking the time to restore my energy.

I was exhausted and drank way too much coffee just to stay awake and function. I was prescribed a sleeping pill to help me sleep because it felt like my body forgot how to calm itself down in order to fall asleep. It took me several years to learn how to prioritize sleep, and when I did, I felt like a new person.

Learning to pay attention to your body's cues—like noticing when you are feeling tired, hungry, or cranky—will help you realize when rest is needed. Our bodies are intelligent, and if we pay attention to them, they will tell us exactly what they need.

Take breaks when you can. Having a twenty-minute power nap or a break from activity may be all you need to revive yourself. At first this might feel like you are wasting time by sleeping in the middle of the day, but naps are great and restorative, especially if you need to stay up later and know you won't survive without some rest beforehand. By giving yourself permission to nap, you are allowing your body to get the rest it needs.

Our bedrooms should be treated with care. This is the one room in your home that should invite and encourage peaceful sleep. Make sure that you have good sleeping conditions, which includes keeping your phone out of the bedroom, limiting screen time before bed and trying to go to bed at the same time each night.

REST AND RELAXATION

If you are having trouble falling asleep or finding time for rest, here are some tips to help you:

- Prioritize your "to-do" list and remove anything that is non-essential or that is just a time filler.

- Meditate to help calm your mind and welcome in peace.

- Keep your phone out of your bedroom. If you use it as an alarm, buy an alarm clock instead.

- Allow yourself to nap when needed.

- Limit screen time before bed. Studies show that the light from our screens can suppress the hormone melatonin, which helps us fall asleep.

- Keep a journal near your bed and write down your worries or gratitude thoughts before bed to get them out of your head and onto paper.

- Try to keep a consistent bedtime.

When we prioritize sleep and rest, we are taking care of ourselves at the most basic level. Our minds and bodies require rest, and depriving ourselves of this basic need is ignoring self-care. When we are tired, we aren't able to focus, make sound judgements, or be present in the moment.

These are just a few things that you can do to welcome more rest into your life. Try them and find the ones that work best for you. Perhaps create a nightly routine where your mind and body get ready for bed and sleep becomes a welcome part of your day.

> When we allow our energy to be restored, we can go from running on empty to feeling more vibrant and alive.

"If you're willing to listen to, be guided by, that still small voice that is the G.P.S. within yourself—to find out what makes you come alive—you will be more than okay."

—OPRAH WINFREY

STILLNESS
&
THE ART OF
SOLITUDE

There is a big difference between loneliness and solitude. Being alone takes on the meaning that you give to it. The difference is in yearning versus contentment. Lonely breeds longing and roots itself in loss. Solitude breeds stillness and is rooted in contentment.

Solitude is a place where we can feed our souls.

Loneliness occurs when we feel removed from things that are familiar—love, family, friends, and proximity. When our hearts are broken, loneliness is augmented. Being alone is sometimes where we need to be. In this space, we can learn to search within and calm our minds. The isolation is necessary to fully embrace what the universe has in store for us.

When I look back on times of loneliness and heartache, I realize that if I did not have that great, lonely discomfort, I could possibly still find myself in a whirlwind of chaos and sorrow.

I learned to appreciate stillness and I began to hear my intuition and notice what my soul had been trying to tell me. My intuitive sense was dulled when I held onto my pain, and I was not practicing the gift that was inside me. I started exercising my intuition and appreciating the fabric of my soul. And what was once the loneliest time of my life soon became one of the richest times of my life.

Without this solitude, I would not have taken the time to search my soul to get back to myself. I realized my identity was tied to a person and a job and that I had lost my authenticity. I had a choice to wallow or grow.

Embracing growth is difficult, but we learn so much about ourselves and the differences between loneliness and solitude when we open up to solitude. Learning to turn loneliness into solitude requires noticing the differences of each. Some of the differences include:

LONELINESS

Depletes our energy and is fueled by sadness. Loneliness is able to permeate when we base our happiness on another. This is a state of contraction and longing. Anxiety and depression will visit more often. Discontentment fuels sorrow and perpetuates the feeling of isolation.

SOLITUDE

Re-energizes. Allows happiness to come from within. Solitude creates space for growth and the state of expansion and contentment. Meditation and prayer become daily routines. We begin to find comfort in times of solitude because we start to enjoy our own company.

The more the beauty of solitude is fostered, the more peace will be found where anxiety used to reside. Learning to tap into our intuition and waiting for answers and inspiration reconnects us to our souls, and our spiritual connection then has room to blossom. When we begin to enjoy solitude, the anxious part of us that feared loneliness melts into being comfortable with ourselves.

Through this lesson, we learn to be compassionate towards our loneliness in order to foster the state of solitude. Without a compassionate approach, we will become stuck and not able to welcome growth. All things deserve compassion and understanding, including our mindsets.

Being alone can be a gift. When you find yourself feeling lonely, pay attention to what it is that you feel is lacking, for instance, if your happiness is tied to another person. If this is the case, begin to redirect the energy and power you are giving to that person onto yourself. Turn your attention to your needs and do the work to find ways to meet them. We can't rely on another person to provide our happiness.

In solitude, we find the peace that comes with accepting ourselves and enjoying our own company. Then we can fully show up in our relationships, rich in the sense of knowing who we are and what we need and do the same for others.

Inviting stillness into your everyday life will reveal the gift of solitude.

To embrace solitude, it is important to put away our electronic devices. We may feel the urge to pull them out as they have become a source of comfort to most of us. True solitude requires the absence of outside influence and our phones provide an escape from that.

At first, it might feel odd to be alone with your own thoughts without the usual everyday distractions but learning to be still and enjoy your own company is beneficial for your mind, body, and soul. Stillness provides answers that we cannot see when we are constantly connected and distracted. How will we know what we really want or even who we really are if we don't take the time to enjoy solitude?

One of the gifts that solitude provides is the time to do the things you always want to do but never seem to find enough time to do. When we allow ourselves to spend time alone, we can do whatever we want. Make a list of all the things you have wanted to do but never get around to, then start working down this list when you have time alone.

After a while, you will find yourself desiring solitude because it provides a sense of calm and a reset from everything that is thrown your way. When you create this space for yourself, offer yourself gratitude for allowing the time to slow down, reconnect with your soul, and recharge your inner glow.

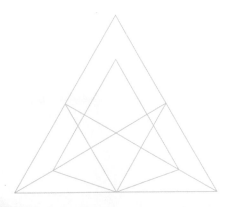

"Intuition: that fabulous gift that is given whole at birth, into every soul, into every being on earth."

—CLARISSA PINKOLA ESTÉS

TRUST
YOURSELF

Have you ever felt like you needed to do something that you didn't particularly want to do? This can feel like a dull ache that will only grow if you keep ignoring it. You will even come up with reasons for ignoring this ache as long as you can, but in the end it's just a list of bad excuses. Our intuition is incessant with its messages. When something is truly important, and we are in tune with our soul, we can't help but hear the messages. The hard part is heeding to them, especially when we don't want to. This is where trust comes into play.

Sometimes the hardest things are the most rewarding.

I made the decision to quit my job after I heard a message loud and clear: "It is time to leave." This scared me because I knew it was true. I had been feeling my intuition's prodding for months. I felt this truth in my heart. Every time I struggled, that feeling in my heart persisted.

It took me five months to muster up the courage to resign. During those five months, my ego tried to reason with my soul, reminding me of the security the job provided to where I almost stayed. But my intuition continued to remind me that it was time to go. Only when I trusted my intuition and quieted my mind from trying to keep me in the safety of the job did I feel free. When I look back, it is interesting that I placed income at a higher importance than following a path that my intuition was pushing me towards.

The universe is very gracious in delivering subtle signs when we need just a little nudge.

This grace is like the loving hand of a parent helping a child cross the street. Making a change and taking a leap can feel like crossing something, however, some leaps can feel like an ocean passage and not a crosswalk. When we decide to leave our security and venture into the unknown, it can feel as if we are about to hit some rough waters when we release what we deem as our source of security.

When our intuition speaks, it can sometimes feel like a gentle nudge and other times the signs are unavoidable. Having a lack of faith in ourselves discounts that everything is always taken care of. In a state of resistance and despair it is hard to see that the answers have always been there. There have been times when our needs have been taken care of before we even realize the need, or just in time, when the feeling of hopelessness takes over. But the answers have always been there, deep inside waiting for us to discover them.

Sometimes our resistance keeps us from tapping into our intuitive center where the answers live, because trusting is an act of release. In our resistance, we find comfort, because the unknown is not easy. When we hold onto things that are never meant to be, it creates so much resistance and pain. When we trust our intuition, we let go and have faith that everything is already working itself out.

Learning to trust your intuition is one of the most rewarding lessons. Being able to trust yourself delivers the greatest sense of calm and clarity. When we quiet our need to control, we renew peace and hope and brighten our spirits.

YOUR INTUITION

Our minds like to take over and reason most
of the time. Being able to quiet your mind and find
stillness can help you tap into your intuition. To begin,
here are a few steps to identify your intuitive cues:

- Recall a time when you felt something in your gut or heard a message loud and clear. What was the message? How did your body respond to the message?

- Think about something that is obviously a "no" answer. Where do you feel that no?

- Then think about something that is obviously a "yes" and notice where you feel that "yes" in your body. Some people feel it in their chests or pit of their stomach, others have feelings in their heads or arms.

Listening to your intuition takes some practice. Our intuition is our soul's way of speaking to us. Each of us has intuitive signals that are always present that we can learn to pay attention to.

Practice noticing where your intuitive cues come from, and then when faced with decisions it becomes easier to pay attention to your intuition.

Your intuition will send you cues through your body and being able to identify them and understand their messages is freeing.

The need to control will dissipate because you will trust yourself, knowing that your intuition—your soul's connection to the universe—is looking out for your best interests and needs.

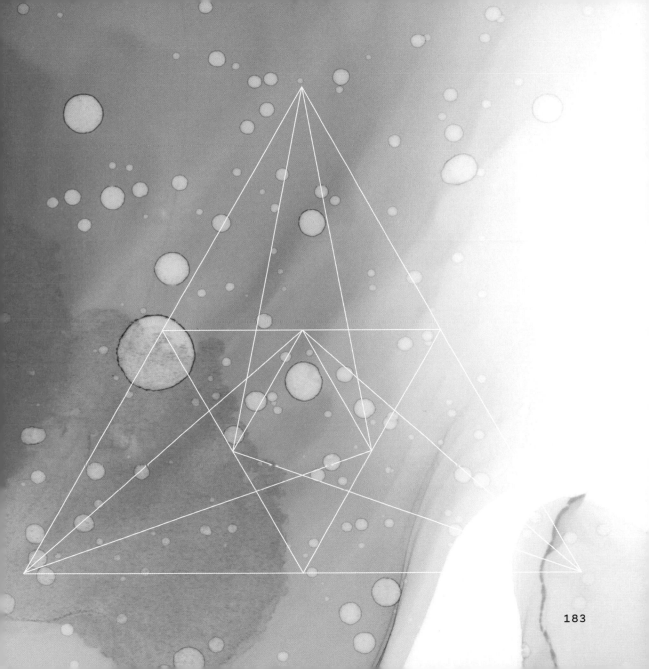

"We must have perseverance and above all confidence in ourselves. We must believe that we are gifted for something and that this thing must be attained."

—MARIE CURIE

Understand Your Worth

One of the keys to creating an abundant life is to know and understand your worth. Whether you are negotiating a salary, setting up pricing for clients, are in a relationship or dating, it is important to know what you want, what you deserve, and, most of all, that you believe it. By understanding and knowing your worth, you send out a signal that you feel worthy.

Worthiness comes from understanding that you are good enough and deserving of wonderful things.

Don't back down and compromise just to make others happy. You are valuable, and in order to get what you deserve, you have to know your value. This doesn't mean that you need to be a bulldozer or demanding, as worthiness nurtures grace and acceptance in oneself and others. Understanding your worth comes from soul work and embracing yourself exactly as you are.

It can be hard to embrace worthiness, especially if there is pain around feeling worth it or feeling that you are enough. This space creates the perfect place to start. Taking some time to address the wounds that made you feel less than and doing the work to let them go either through forgiveness, therapy, or journaling brings immense healing. There is no need to hold on to the pain that compromises your feelings of worth.

Remind yourself, "I am enough," a phrase I must tell myself often.

One day, after an argument, I received a text from my husband that said, "You are enough." As I read these words from a man who saw what was actually going on in my heart, I felt loved and secure. He sees my heart and knows my story and can dig deeper than the surface to see that the insecure part of me was crying out for certainty. I felt seen and knew I needed to offer myself grace. All I could do in that moment was offer myself gratitude for the gift of love that entered into my life because I am enough and worthy of love and acceptance.

Someone saw me as enough. I felt worthy, but I recognized that I needed to heal the wound inside of me where I still felt that I wasn't worthy. To heal, I needed to go back to some painful memories and offer my younger self love, compassion, and acceptance. I was then able to understand that my worth and value had been there all along.

We all have moments in our lives where we have been hurt. Sometimes the pain makes us feel so unworthy that we can hold on to it and start to believe that we are not enough. These wounds are deep but can be healed. We have the ability to go back to each scenario, painful as it may be, and offer our younger selves the love and compassion they so desperately needed at that moment.

Your Worthiness

Begin by recalling the moments when you were made
to feel less than, not enough, and unworthy.

- Go back to who you were then
and ask, "What do I need?"

- When you hear the answer, offer
compassion and love. Say the
words you desperately needed
to hear in that moment.

- Repeat the mantras, "I am
enough and worthy of love," and
"I offer myself the grace to heal
from this wound and release all
the pain I've held on to."

A wound can heal with proper care.

When we go back to each scenario where we needed love and compassion, we begin to heal wounds that have kept us from understanding our worth. Even though you didn't have the tools back then to heal, you can offer the gift of acceptance now.

Once we work on healing the wounds that keep us from accepting what we deserve, we can then move on to dealing with scarcity, which is another block to truly embracing our worth.

Scarcity is the root of not feeling enough. It is easy to fall into a scarcity mindset when things don't fall into place exactly how or when we want them to. We can get upset with ourselves and control creeps in and augments the need, making us feel scarce. But if the situation is truly evaluated from a place of calm, you are always enough.

To understand your worth, ask yourself where you don't feel enough. Question your beliefs around money and worthiness. See if there is a belief that is lying dormant that comes up in times of scarcity. In times of uncertainty, instead of shying away from abundance, move towards it by facing the fear-based thoughts and noticing where they originate, then accept that you are always worthy and always enough.

Even if you are trying to create abundance in your life and feel like there isn't enough, remind yourself that there is always enough. Don't compare yourself to where you think you should be or to other people's journeys.

Your worth is not tied to a goal or perception.

When self-doubt and negative talk seem to run a loop in your brain, interrupt the pattern by simply stating, "I am enough!" When we are able to release scarcity, we can move towards feeling enough and from there arrive in abundance. The moment we embrace that we are enough and have enough, contentment can take root.

Self-love and contentment with who we are right now is so important. Meet yourself where you are today. Don't live in past mistakes and failures, do the work to heal them. Own where you are and love yourself wholly and completely. From this place of acceptance, you can embrace your worth and your value will radiate from within.

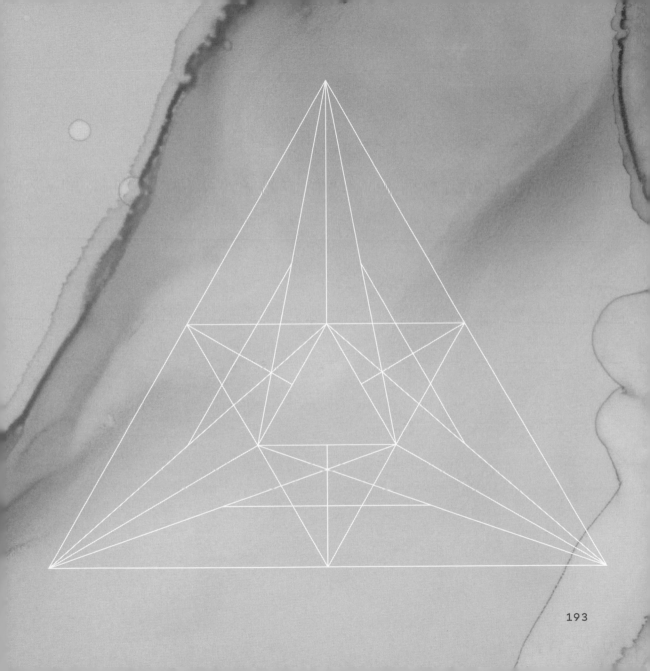

"I have learned that as long as I hold fast to my beliefs and values—and follow my own moral compass—then the only expectations I need to live up to are my own."

—MICHELLE OBAMA

Values
Are Your
Foundation

Discovering and defining your core values is essential to creating more meaning in your life. Values are the foundational beliefs and ways to think and act that are most important to you. They are what we want to emulate in our day-to-day life—the non-negotiable feelings we desire.

After taking the time to answer the questions on page 197, come up with your top five core values. This is a living document that evolves as you learn and grow. There are usually one or two that stay the same throughout our lives.

In order to narrow it down to five, look at your answers for questions one, four, and five. These are clues to what is most important to you. Make a list, then sit down and find your top five.

Once you have decided on your top five, you now have the framework for how you want to feel and act. If your life is currently void of these values, see if you can infuse them. If the answer is "no," begin looking for careers, people, and communities that align with your values.

There have been times when I allowed my equilibrium to falter because I lost balance trying to please others because one of my core values is connection. However, connection does not mean being a doormat.

Your Values

Noticing and removing what keeps you from being who you want to be is the first step in seeking alignment with your values. Be open to what comes up. Don't force the answers to appear. Sometimes we need to slough off layers of years of frustration in our lives in order to truly uncover the answers. In order to discover your values, here are a few questions to ask yourself:

1. What do I stand for?

2. What am I doing when I am at my best?

3. What qualities do I admire in others?

4. What do I believe in?

5. What attributes do I want to display in my life?

I value genuine, heartfelt connection that comes in the form of quality time and reciprocal compassion and love. When I try to please others, masking it as connection, I step out of my values in order to be everything to everyone. The pendulum swings back and forth and I find myself feeling lost in the middle of everything.

Learn to recognize the moments when you need to say "no" to allow for the right "yes" to occur.

This can be difficult, especially when building a business, trying to find a relationship, planning a move, or in any big life decision. But the desire to be in your best possible mindset requires that you heed to this lesson in order to show up correctly in business and in life.

It can be tempting to try to accommodate each request, but continuously returning to your values will remind you what you truly want to create. If it doesn't serve your purpose or goal, decide whether or not to say "no." Being clear on your values will make the tough "no" easier because you will know that it moves you closer to where you want to go.

When we are living in our values, it doesn't take as much effort to do things because at our core we are aligned. Being aligned is a sweet spot and is quite accessible once you identify your values. Think about a time when you felt like everything seemed to flow, a time when you didn't have to struggle. Notice what values were being expressed at that time.

If you are finding it difficult to remember such a moment, think about a time when everything seemed like a struggle, a time when no matter what you did, it felt like nothing was working out. In that moment, notice if you were honestly living in your values. Were your thoughts and actions aligned with your values? What were you feeling?

Sometimes the opposite of the negative emotions that we feel can lead us closer to our values. For instance, when we find ourselves constantly feeling scattered and being frustrated because of it, it may be that focus or clarity is one of our desired values.

Once you identify your values, the next step is to incorporate them into your daily life.

Ask yourself "How can I
incorporate my values today?"
when you start your day or
sit down at your desk.

I like to have mine written out in a place where I can easily see
them. This is a great reminder for me and helps me stay aligned.

As you incorporate your values into your life, you will find a new
flow to the things you do and an ease in saying "no" to things that
don't align with them. When we feel aligned with our soul, we shine
brighter and attract more opportunities to live our best lives.

"I have learned to live each day as it comes, and not to borrow trouble by dreading tomorrow."

—DOROTHEA DIX

WORRY LESS

Worry robs us of our joy and can leave us feeling dissatisfied and full of anxiety. When we focus on what we don't have or what is going wrong, we are taking our focus away from the present moment. This is when scarcity creeps in and grabs a hold with force. What might have been something that we are completely grateful for can turn into our greatest frustration.

How does this happen? Expectations—they create disappointment and rob the joy from something that has the possibility to create excitement.

When frustration takes over, we start to notice all the things that could and have gone wrong.

The more we focus on what could go wrong, the more we change the energy around the entire situation and actually attract negativity to it.

This is where scarcity takes over, because it sees the perfect opportunity to sweep in and make a nice home inside our negative thoughts and emotions, causing them to be augmented. Thoughts of not being enough, doing enough, or having enough, seep in and before we know it, we regret the thing that we wanted so badly.

Placing such high expectations on the things you want the most can lead to sabotaging their success. We place expectations in relationships, at work, in family, and even in working out. Sometimes our need for perfection and control can flare up when we get attached to outcomes that we deem necessary for success, and then—POOF! —it falls apart, leaving us in a whirlwind of anxiety.

It can take us time to come to the realization that our own expectations of perfection can lead to feelings of anxiety. In the meantime, we can be left in a disgruntled state wondering, "Why?!", "How did this happen once again?" and placing blame everywhere we can until we realize that we are in control over the way we perceive each situation and the expectations we set. Feelings of anxiety can justify negative thoughts because we can dwell on the past pain and project it into the future.

It is hard to let go of expectations. We want what we want when we want it. Best-laid plans are just that, plans. Nothing is set in stone and so many things can happen that are out of our control. When we decide that things need to be a certain way and leave little room for variety, we set ourselves up for disappointment.

There is a way to replace scarcity with abundance and worry less. It takes some work, but with practice you can change the way you react and replace anxiety with positive feelings and reactions.

Release the expectation, attachment, and need for control. Be fluid and allow things to occur as they will.

Reframe the negative thought or feeling with something positive. Ask yourself: "What is going right?"

Recognize what is going right with gratitude. The best way to go from scarcity to abundance is gratitude. Always look for the positive and be grateful. This tiny step will change your mindset and the way you think because you will begin to look for the good in each situation.

Notice where scarcity has created frustration in your life and take the time to heal this wound. Our bodies have a physical response to this emotion. We crave security and fulfillment. When we are off balance in this area, we feel anxious, scarce, and controlling.

CULTIVATE
POSITIVE ENERGY

Transforming our energy frees up the tension that we hold
physically and emotionally so that we can heal with gratitude.
Here are a couple of exercises to help transform your anxious
energy and invite in positive and grateful energy:

1. Stand with your feet hip distance apart and feel yourself grounding into the Earth. Hold your arms by your side, palms facing outward. Close your eyes and release any tension through your feet into the Earth and through your hands. "I release what no longer serves me and offer gratitude for the blessings in my life."

2. Sit down with your back straight and feet on the ground. Close your eyes and focus on your breath. Take big breaths from your diaphragm, extending your belly. Count to ten (one – breathe in, two – breathe out). Repeat until you find yourself in the present moment.

3. Think about a time when you felt abundant; when you realized that your needs were met. Take a moment to feel that sensation throughout your body. Root yourself into this and bring yourself back to it when scarcity takes over.

When we are out of balance, not only do we emotionally feel pain, but our bodies also respond. We can hold on to the negative feelings and scarce thoughts and store them as pain in our bodies.

By creating the sensation of being grounded and present, we can release the anxiety and fear that surrounds the situation. Trust that all your needs are always provided for. Bring yourself into the present moment and recognize that your fears are based on a projection into the future, distracting you from the right here, right now. When we release fears, we can allow our inner glow to shine brighter and move forward with a sense of peace.

Gratitude can heal where anxiety and scarcity once scarred.

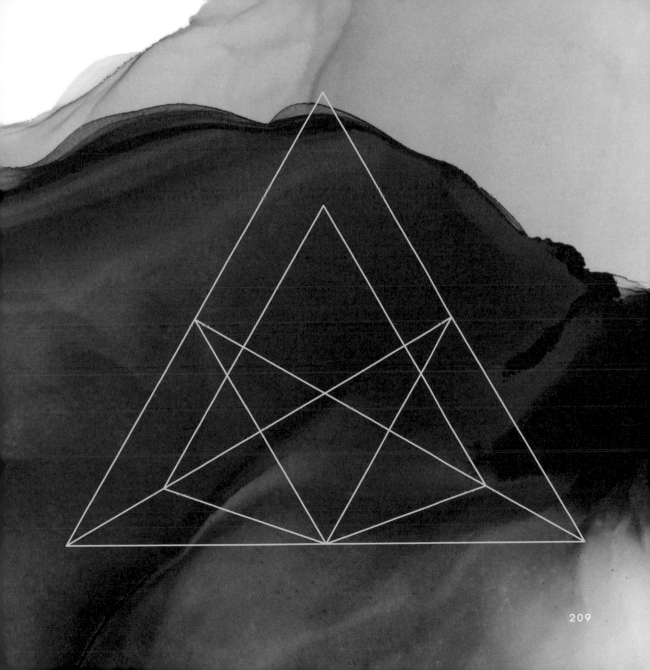

"We are what we think. All that we are arises with our thoughts. With our thoughts, we make the world."

—BUDDHA

eXamine
Your
Thoughts

Our thoughts have so much power and create our reality. What we think about creates a vibrational energy that attracts like energy to us. If our thoughts are negative, we feel low and our energy matches our thoughts. In this state, it is easy to focus on the negative and notice when there is something to be negative about. Like energy is attracted to us and we find others to commiserate with because they have similar frequencies as us.

On the other hand, when our thoughts are positive and abundant, similar energy is attracted to us as well. From this place, we access our inner glow, which operates at a high vibrational frequency. For instance, the act of practicing gratitude brings more things to be grateful for because it is a higher vibration and our thoughts are calibrated to gratitude and not misery. When we are operating at a higher frequency and our thoughts are calibrated to positivity and joy, we attract positivity and others are drawn to us.

If you want to change your thoughts and raise your vibration, examine your thoughts and reframe the negative thought patterns.

To begin, notice when your thoughts are bringing you down. Lower vibrations feel low. Examples of these types of thoughts are judgements, negative self-talk, and anxious and depressing thoughts. Since our minds have the power to create our reality, if we dwell on the thoughts that bring us down, we will stay there.

I came home one day to a notice of my rent being raised. Although this isn't the best news to receive, I was surprised by my reaction. My immediate thought was that everything is as it should be, and everything will be okay. I had been working hard on reframing negative thoughts and finding the good in each situation.

I decided to go for a run and headed to the beach. I was thinking about the rent notice when suddenly two whales tails rose out of the water very close to shore. I stopped, stunned at what I had just witnessed. Soon I realized that there were actually four whales swimming close to shore.

The only word that came to mind was, "abundance."

I often scan the water in search for whales, seals, and dolphins when I am on the beach. I usually see one occasionally, out in the distance. But this time, I was being shown just how abundant the universe really is. I considered this a good omen, one of abundance and provision.

By adopting a positive mindset that everything is going to be okay, we can change the energy we bring. Think about a time when the universe provided in ways you could not have even imagined. It is at times like these that we are reminded of the lesson of going from a mindset of scarcity to sufficiency and finally abundance.

If we allow thoughts of scarcity to overtake us, scarcity becomes our reality. Fixing our minds towards abundance and going a step further and practicing gratitude for abundance all around attracts more abundance into our lives. Simply put, this is the law of attraction.

I am continually amazed at how just changing my mindset from scarcity and anxiety to abundance and gratitude changes everything. Letting go and noticing the positive is the most important step in changing the energy around negative thoughts. Our brains have plasticity and can be changed with practice. Training our mind to find the positive recalibrates it, so that it becomes easier over time.

If there are feelings that are being harbored around a certain person or situation, you can transform the energy you give and receive. The story you tell yourself about the situation may perpetuate negative emotions and thoughts. Think about a way that you can reframe the narrative in a more positive or healing light.

One of the things that has always helped me when I get stuck in a spiral is remembering that everyone is operating from their level of understanding. They may be in pain and unable to consider both sides. This empathic approach helps alleviate the feeling of needing to be understood and to be right—even if you are right.

Then there are cases when you just need to let go and walk away because the other person is just too hurtful. If they are unable to reach past their pain and they continue to create pain and suffering in your life, it may be time to release them.

Speaking and living your truth takes courage.

It is not always easy to say the things that need to be said or even to let go and walk away. Remember that everything is energy.

All the energy that is being stored can be released in a loving way. Think about a time when you found the courage to speak the truth and how relieved you felt. That was a release of powerful energy.

When we examine our thoughts and notice the energy we emit, it is easier to reframe thought patterns and change the energy. Unless we become conscious of how our mind is operating, we will unknowingly keep our energy and thoughts at a lower frequency.

Raise your vibration and examine your thoughts.

Replace old thought patterns with a new positive outlook and become a beacon for abundance.

CULTIVATE

A POSITIVE MINDSET

If there is negative energy surrounding an area in
your life, ask the following questions:

- Is there anything I
  need to say or come to
  terms with?

- Is there a situation or
  relationship that needs
  attention or maybe even
  less attention?

- What meaning am I giving
  this situation?

- How can I release
  the energy around
  this situation?

"Though it seems curious,
I do not remember ever asking
for anything but what I got it.
And I always received it as an
answer to my prayers."

—SOJOURNER TRUTH

YIELD TO THE UNIVERSE

Holding on to something tightly that isn't there is useless and controlling. When we try to generate an outcome that seems forced, we create an unrealistic expectation, fueled by stress and anxiety.

The universe knows our deepest desires. Our thoughts, prayers, and visualizations are paid attention to. When we try to force things to happen, we feel stressed and anxious. When we yield to the process and trust the universe, we enter a state of flow and things work out exactly as they are meant to.

Several years ago, I went through a career transition. Before I became a life coach, I had transitioned from banking into the wine industry, which was completely new and exciting to me. I didn't know much about the industry, but I knew that I needed to allow things to happen and learn as much as I could instead of living in fear.

I was terrified when I let go, I thought that if I held on for just a bit longer, things would fall into place. I was used to security and certainty and yielding to the unknown was unnerving to me.

When I surrendered to the experience and the lessons that were meant to be learned, everything started to fall into place.

I found a mentor who helped me navigate the industry and my career and in the years with that company I traveled all over the world to places I had only dreamed of and stretched my brain beyond the capacity I thought possible.

All of this happened despite my need to control; because I allowed myself to go with the flow and surrender. If I had tried to control the situation and work it out to what I thought was possible, I would have never known that I could learn as much as I did nor see parts of the world I had only dreamed of seeing. The universe knew exactly what I needed and what I was capable of.

When it feels like you are being blindly led, allow trust to take place.

The act of surrender is not giving up, it is an act of trust. This is a sacred place within the soul—a deep, vulnerable place to enter. To let the walls down around the heart and to open the soul to a possibility that can't be seen is raw, yet absolutely exciting and brave.

When we surrender and trust that everything will be alright, we can be pleasantly surprised by the grace of the universe. Situations that seem hopeless when in our control are completely turned around when we let go of the reigns. The universe lovingly allows us the time to realize we need to let go, and when we do, that's where the miracles happen.

What we can't see holds a gift if we allow it to happen. It is amazing when things are revealed after the act of trust. What we think we need or want is always replaced by something perfect and sometimes greater than we can imagine. With each act of surrender, we learn that the universe really does have our backs and listens to all the desires of our hearts.

TRUST AND LEARN TO SURRENDER

It takes less effort to let go than it does to hold on to something that is not meant to be. Stress levels will drop. The relief will be amazing and allowing life to unfold as it should will bring greater joy. If you are struggling with trusting and yielding to something you can't see, try this exercise in release:

- Imagine whatever it is you are trying to control is in the palm of your hand.

- Make a fist and hold it as tightly as you can.

- Feel the tension in your arm and anywhere else in your body as you try your best to keep your fist gripping onto this desired object or outcome.

- Slowly release your grip, one finger at a time, feeling the release as you open your fist.

- Take a deep breath and let go, noticing the release of tension throughout your hand, your arm, and body.

- Say this mantra: "I release my need to control and I yield to the universe. I trust that whatever comes next is for my highest good."

Think about a time when you were worried about an outcome and how things actually worked out despite all the fear and anxiety. The universe always provides a solution. When we yield to the universe and trust, we remove a burden from our mind and soul knowing that we don't have to do it alone.

The illusion of control keeps us trapped and dims our inner glow. We shine brighter when our spirits are free. When we imagine our fist held tightly we realize that all it holds is the air and creates tension within the body. When we let go of our grasp, we notice the release of tension and free-flowing air around each finger. Nothing fell out of the palm, because there was nothing to grasp.

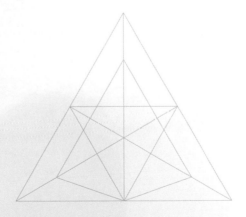

"I urge you to try and create the world you want to live in. Minister to the world in a way that can change it. Minister radically in a real, active, practical, get your hands dirty way."

—CHIMAMANDA NGOZI ADICHIE

ZERO IN
ON WHAT
YOU WANT

Figuring out what you really want and then taking action to achieve it is one of the most empowering things you can do for yourself.

When you take time to answer the question, "What do I want?" you equip yourself with a goal to work towards.

With everything that gets in the way, it is easy to get caught up in minor details of life and ignore our true desires. Taking time to zero in on what you want helps you gain clarity and direction in life.

A great place to begin is to think about what you wanted to be when you grew up. What did you want to emulate as a child? As an adult, did you tuck away your dream to pursue a path that made sense at the time but wasn't what your soul longed for?

When you look back, there might be actions and choices that always supported your dream but were deemed less important as life happened. Sometimes we choose a "viable" career or a relationship that seems like a good idea only to leave us to feel empty or unfulfilled. These feelings persist the longer we ignore our true desires.

If you veer away from your dream for long enough, it will come back to remind you. After years of feeling unfulfilled, you need to take the time to ask yourself, "What do I *really* want?" The answer might not come immediately, but sit with the question for some time. When the answer reveals itself, it is like a lightbulb that has long been turned off being reignited.

After you know the answer to your question, begin to take steps towards making the dream come true. You may not know where to start, but there are coaches, mentors, classes, and books out there to help you take the first step. Empower yourself with knowledge and begin.

You don't have to know all the answers right away. When you have a goal in mind, there are several steps that need to take place to get to the finish line.

It's even okay to take baby steps because every step forward counts. I didn't know the first thing about becoming an author, so I did what I thought would be a good start and started a blog. My first blog was about my adventures and a way to chronicle where I've been. The more I wrote, the more I became comfortable with my voice and I found each post liberating. I became more serious about my goal and just kept creating content, not knowing who was reading my words but knowing that I *had* to write. Eventually things fell into place when they were supposed to. When I began, I didn't know that each step would lead to where I am now, but I am grateful for each step, lesson, and milestone.

When we take steps towards our dreams, the universe meets us where we are to support our efforts.

When we zero in on what we want and take action, we get in the flow and nothing else seems to matter. That is when fulfillment can occur. When the answer arrives, be grateful. Don't back down. Take whatever step you need to get started. There will be mistakes and you may fall down a few times, but knowing that you are going after what you want helps with getting back up.

Think about an entrepreneur and the emotions he or she goes through in one day. There is joy, achievement, failure, pride, loss, contentment, and gratitude. Some may quit because it is a lot to deal with, but the ones who stay the course ride the wave because they have their eye on the goal and keep their vision close by. They might correct their course from time to time, but the vision helps them show up and do the work required of them. Remember that once you decide to take action on what you want, the universe will meet you there. You will not have to figure everything out on your own. Your soul already knows the path. It may not be the way you expect it, but keep showing up for your dream. Build resilience around rejection because there is a "yes" somewhere waiting to happen.

PURPOSE AND FULFILLMENT

Finding your flow and staying true to your vision will keep you grounded and motivated. To zero in on what you want, take these steps:

- Think about what you wanted to be when you were a child. This may hold a clue to what you really want now.

- Take the time to sit with the question "What do I want?" Don't force the answer, let it come to you naturally.

- When you hear the answer, take action.

- If you aren't sure how to take action, find someone to help you; a coach, a friend, a teacher, a trainer. I hired a coach to help me write my first book. I've coached people who have completely changed their careers and started businesses that they always wanted to, but never knew where to start. The point is, there is help out there and you don't have to do this alone.

You never know who is reading, watching, listening, or willing to collaborate. Stay committed and put in the work. If you continue to show up for your dream, it is amazing what can happen.

Keep dreaming and working towards what you want. Don't let difficulties stop you from achieving your greatness. The most magnificent accomplishments start with the spark of a dream and then, with work and faith, they are accomplished.

When you are working towards your dreams, you are living with intention. Living intentionally creates a life of purpose and fulfillment. Take steps to live your best life and you will feel a brilliance from within that is impossible for others to ignore.

Now glow brightly and shine your light everywhere you go!

The world is a brighter and better place because you are in it.

"She is so bright and glorious that you cannot look at her face or her garments for the splendor with which she shines. For she is terrible with the terror of the avenging lightning, and gentle with the goodness of the bright sun."

—HILDEGARD VON BINGEN

GLOW ON

When I was thinking about what to include in this book, I thought about the struggles that seemed to continually show up in coaching and in life. There are many things that can dim our light, many of which we aren't aware of. I chose the common themes that I have heard about and dealt with over the past several years.

There was a time when I allowed things to dim my glow because I gave my power away to outside influences. I was left feeling drained. From this place, I was unable to see that I was allowing my light to be dimmed. I was afraid that my light was too bright for others. I noticed that I downplayed things so that others would feel comfortable.

I wanted to be vibrant and feel alive and in order to do that, I had to pay attention to where my energy was being drained. This was hard for me because I had to let go of old patterns and thoughts that I held on to for years. In letting go, I was able to shine and find comfort in allowing my beautiful, brilliant light to illuminate places I had ignored. I was no longer afraid to shine.

My hope is that these chapters have helped you create a new awareness of your inner glow and showed you how to mindfully calibrate your light. Your light is always with you and it never goes out. There will be times when you feel like it has been dimmed, but you have the power to shine brighter. Once you are able to find your glow, you can access the switch to brighten what was dimmed at any time.

Never, ever dim your light to make others feel comfortable. We need your brilliance. You are meant to shine bright.

The second part of this journey is to make sure that you continually feed your soul. When we focus on listening to what we truly need and take the time for self-care, we ensure our glow shines brighter. This is a mindful journey of listening to the cues of our mind, body, and soul.

Your soul is beautiful. Be kind to yourself and feed your soul to keep your energy high and aware. As you raise your vibration, you will become a beacon for others and inspire them to also shine their lights brighter. It's time that we claim the power we have within us to cultivate a vibrant life full of joy and purpose. It's time that we light up this world with our brilliance.

Glow on, glow up, and glow brighter!

ACKNOWLEDGEMENTS

I want to thank Rage Kindelsperger, my publishing fairy godmother. Thank you for seeing something in my writing and offering me the opportunity to make my dream come true. Words will never describe how grateful I am for you.

Thank you to my editor, Keyla Pizarro-Hernández, for taking the time to help me elevate my writing and for helping me get this manuscript where it needed to be.

To my husband, Nate, thank you for being so supportive and for always being my biggest fan. Your love and support are more than I could have ever imagined.

To my family, thank you for reading my words since I started writing stories as a child and supporting my dream of becoming a writer.

To my Glow Tribe, thank you for spreading the word enthusiastically and being the epitome of collaboration. You glow so brightly!

To my readers, thank you for choosing to read my words when there are so many words to choose from. I appreciate your time and attention and am grateful for your support.